The Khakee Ressalah

The Khakee Ressalah

Service & Adventure with the Meerut
Volunteer Horse During the Indian
Mutiny 1857-58

Robert Henry Wallace Dunlop

LEONAUR

The Khakee Ressalah: Service & Adventure with the Meerut Volunteer Horse
During the Indian Mutiny 1857-58

Originally published in 1858 under the
title Service and Adventure with the Khakee Ressalah.

Published by Leonaur Ltd

Material original to this edition and its origination in
this form copyright © 2005 Leonaur Ltd

ISBN (10 digit): 1-84677-017-3 (hardcover)
ISBN (13 digit): 978-1-84677-017-3 (hardcover)

ISBN (10 digit): 1-84677-009-2 (softcover)
ISBN (13 digit): 978-1-84677-009-8 (softcover)

http://www.leonaur.com

Publishers Notes

Contents

for Military Aid, "Not a Man Available" – Death of Mr.
Johnston, The Officiating District Officer – A Fortnight's
Incumbency by Mr. T———.

Chapter Five p.51

Chapter Six p.59

Chapter Seven p.71

Chapter Eight p.75

Chapter Nine p.89

Preface

At the commencement of the year I had determined on writing a brief historical sketch of the Meerut Mutiny, and the various phases of the disturbances during 1857, under the belief that the general history of this most important epoch in our British Indian annals might best be hereafter attained, by combining such threads of narrative drawn by separate writers in every district affected by the revolt. But such a narrative, I was told by a friend who was informed of my intention, would not be acceptable; as few care for learned disquisitions on the Sepoy revolt, its causes, local history, and consequences. Everybody has his own opinion or theory on the matter, and deems it superior to all others. The public infinitely prefer the minutiae of personal adventure to the details of a history probably only locally interesting; and as our Anglo-Indian friends have passed through a strange phase of existence, we should wish to hear from one or two what they thought, saw, and did, as matters of routine.

There was some truth in this;– so, modifying my original intention, I commence the following more egotistical episode, hoping to effect, to some extent, my original object, under the garb of this more ephemeral article, an Anglo-Indian's Journal.

I had retained notes and drafts of my letters, which detailed, truly at least, my own experiences; and there is, I believe, scarcely a more trustworthy record-office, for many truths concealed for history, than such gossiping private letters. We have here been acting history for the last twelve months; we know by personal experience, many of us, what are the facts; and we know, by our own papers from home, what is accepted as fact in England, the deductions therefrom tending to make us believe history in many of its details. A sham fortuitous accident by an Overland Summary paragraph may confer fame; a public speaker in England may transform Colonel Smith of the 75th N.I. (who is really a very ordinary officer) into a Heaven-sent hero; while men like Taylor, Hodson, Metcalfe, Sanford, Wardlow, Robertson, Barnes, Ricketts, &c. are unnoticed and unknown; to remain so, even after brilliant services, if a chance fever or bullet remove them, or future opportunities fail them. What an invaluable record of the real events of the fortnight does not every mail-steamer carry home, if it could only be sifted, condensed, and printed! What bold views in manly characters, what minute stippling and word-painting, in pointed female hands! Doubtless family pride or uxorial folly will sometimes force "Dear Henry" or "Dear George" before the public as heroes, though even less deserving than the "Brook Green Volunteer." I have heard letters much admired at home, read out in this country amidst roars of laughter from those intimate with the circumstances, thus extravagantly distorted to gratify the vanity of, as the writer possibly supposed, a confined family circle, or carefully composed under a moral conviction that they would be "sent to the papers;" but correlative testimony in other correspondence would be a sufficient corrective to any such imposture. Sprightly feminine pencilling, seizing on ordinary incidents, and painting them till the outline is almost destroyed, may unintentionally do mischief, or seriously mislead the press and the public as to private character; but the tout ensemble is a photograph always of some value, though it sometimes makes the sitter unnaturally ugly.

This sketch, then, is not written under any delusion that the writer saw more of adventure than his companions. The scenes he witnessed were the every-day lot of hundreds of our countrymen, and on that account possibly interesting to some of those, whose presence in the midst of the conflict we often earnestly longed for, and whose first impulse on hearing of our condition was, as we read with thrilling hearts in India, "to come out at once and join us."

Meerut, May, 1858.

Chapter One

On the 1st of May, 1857, the writer of this sketch was wandering among the snows and valleys of Himalaya. Having suffered from fever and liver, those scourges of Anglo-Indian existence, I was ordered off to the Hills in April, on the paramount warrant of medical authority, to pass the next six months in a cooler climate than that of Meerut, in which province I held the rank of "Préfet Député," called Deputy Commissioner in the Punjab, or Magistrate and Collector in the ordinary Anglo-Indian vernacular. My companion was Lieutenant Speke, of the 65th N.I., a brother of the intrepid young pioneer for central Africa, who is at present engaged with Captain Burton in exploring that country.

Many conversations had we on the exciting prospect of peril and adventure surrounding him, little dreaming of the eventful era opening to ourselves; – that, surrounded as we then were with the clear cold air of the Hills, amidst primeval forests whose stillness was unbroken for years, save by the cry of a pheasant, or the fall of some patriarchal tree, we should, ere a few months elapsed, be suffering incessant exposure to the sun of the plains, and one of us, admist the storming of Delhi, lying mortaly wounded on its beach. Before we had left the plains no symptoms of disaffection had appeared at Meerut. There was no regular post amid the snowy solitudes of the Himalaya, and all our letters and papers having been ordered to be forwarded to await us in Jummoo, in Cashmere, we shot pheasants and gooral through Kooloo and Sirmoor, utterly ignorant of

A Goorkha, au Naturel

16

the sudden change in the scenes we had so lately left.

On the 31st of May, happening to arrive at the village of Nuggur, near the source of the Beâs river, we met Major Hay, the Assistant Commissioner of Kooloo, with a young officer, on his way to Lahoul on sick leave; from them we learnt of the massacres of Meerut and Delhi, of the rapidly spreading flames of revolt; the aspect of affairs (our misfortunes only reaching us) looked even more gloomy than the reality.

It was evident that the time had really come, of which I had frequently reflected on the possibility, when all who bore the Anglo-Saxon name in this country must join their brethren to defend our supremacy, or die hard in losing it. An order of the Commander-in-Chief to military men on general leave required Speke's immediate return, and, as the few weeks of cool air I had enjoyed had given me, apparently, a fresh lease of life, I deemed the commands of duty equally imperative in my own case: the next morning, therefore, saw us bidding adieu to our hospitable host, Major Hay, and returning by forced marches to the plains.

Our servants were soon too fatigued to keep up with us, and most of our property had to be left at villages en route. Coolies were hardly to be procured for even the smallest bundle of clothes. We had each purchased a tattoo pony at Nuggur, and I, having got a third at Kooloo for my faithful Shikaree Kunhaya, we accomplished a fortnight's journey into Simla in six days.

We had heard much of the great Simla panic; the want of unanimity in the English residents, the want, in fact, of some master-mind to compel obedience to the dictates of necessity in providing for the general safety.

The soldiers of the Nusseeree Battalion had most

unquestionably mutinied, and the station was at one time in danger; but nothing could justify, in Englishmen, that want of presence of mind which abandoned the defence of the English women and children in Simla, by quitting the Bank House at the dictation of the mutineers, and the Station, at that of their own fears. The Nusseeree Battalion does not possess so many of those brave little fellows, the Ghoorkas, as the Simoor and other Hill corps; had there been none but Ghoorkas in the regiment, it is probable no cause for anxiety would have arisen. Many in England seem to class all tribes of Indians together, whereas the Hillmen and Sikhs are less like the Poorbeas than Englishmen are like Russians or the men of European Turkey.

On arriving at Simla, we found the inhabitants either in the hot or cold fit of panic, either nervously excited at the portentous news of revolt almost hourly arriving, or apathetically yielding to the reaction consequent on their late stirring exodus. We entered the news-room opposite the Pavilion hotel, and astonished the quidnuncs of that coterie, by asking, with all the verdancy of men dropt from the moon, questions on events known almost by heart by every European, man, woman, or child, in the Sanitarium. These parish politicians, with such an unusual supply of pabulum, were only too happy to descant, ore rotunda, to such novices as ourselves, on details worn threadbare to the habitues of their circle. Here we rapidly acquainted ourselves with the unredeemed horrors of Meerut, of the 10th May, or the dreary detail of foul treachery and butchery at Delhi, the dismal picture of which was gloriously relieved by a lightning flash across its space, the light struck by young Willoughby, the first hero of our great Indian tragedy, and which roused throughout India the stern devoted spirit that led a handful of Anglo-Saxons to battle with indomitable energy for the supremacy their fathers had won, and which finally planted the colours of England on the shattered site of that daring deed which Willoughby has left us, an heirloom to be treasured in the memories of his countrymen.

I called on a lady of my acquaintance, and received a lively account of the memorable garrisoning of the Bank. Mrs. P——— and her husband had been exceptions to the sadly general exhibition of fright during the Simla panic. Her husband had gone down to take his place where manhood should, and she spoke confidently and cheeringly, as a truehearted Englishwoman ought, of the tremendous task in store for us. She too spoke, as all were speaking, of Lawrence, – Lawrence, who not only got through Herculean labours himself, but sternly forced all maligners to do their duty; who, with the authority of a master mind, flashed message after message of abrupt command wherever the electric shock was necessary. One of the earliest victims of the struggle had sunk, she said, killed by an attack of Lawrence's telegraphic messages.

Chapter Two

The road from Simla to the plains bore frequent testimony to the stirring events enacting below. Soldiers of the Puttialah Rajah, who had declared for the British government, were wandering along the road; commissariat stores were coming up with Sikh escorts; the Dawk bungalow at Kussowlee was occupied by fugitives from Delhi, who were congratulating themselves on their fortunate escapes from the scenes to which we were hurrying. The descent from the cool heights of Kussowlee to the sweltering plains by Kalka could give some idea of "Æneas' visit to the infernal regions."

We found the half-caste managers of the hotel at Kalka sulky to a degree. Cholera was raging on the plains. No carriage to Umballa could at first be procured, and a more unpromising commencement to the campaign than the deadly choking hours passed at Kalka can hardly be conceived. We could not both go with our things in the mail cart; but we at last got out two nondescript vehicles, of which Speke drove one and I the other. What with the series of combats with unbroken horses, and the coming to pieces of one of our vehicles, and other mishaps, indomitable energy alone got us to Umballa.

I had visited the station in its palmy days, and was startled at the change. Long lines of blackened ruins stretched tenantless around us; all the nearest bungalows which were undestroyed were empty. The few natives we saw skulking about appeared scared, and none could inform us where we might find shelter or means to get on with our journey.

Speke had a friend in the station, adjutant of one of the native infantry corps. We at last got to his residence. He laughingly told us they were all in a state of siege; and the incongruous appearance of the church, half filled with supplies, tenanted by a few English soldiers, and surrounded with earthworks and bastions, showed how uncertain the "even tenor of life" was there.

We arranged to push on to Kurnaul the same night, and occupied the interval in visiting the Commissioner, and attending, with our revolvers in our belts, the public execution of a soubadar, jamadar, and pay havildar, three native officers of the 5th Native Infantry, in the presence of the few remaining men of their corps, for "concealment of mutiny." At the residence of the Commissioner we found the Postmaster-General, and the author of "Modern India."

Every packet opened that day had brought news of fresh disasters. They had never had such unpromising accounts, they said, since the mutiny began. The prospect was gloomy enough, and showed badly for those engaged in the present campaign; but though numbers had little hope for themselves individually – and in too many instances have these forebodings ended in the silent quiet of the grave, – yet none with whom I spoke, I am proud to say, ever for a moment dreamt for England of aught but final triumph and victory, fully trusting that, even should it please Providence that the present representatives of our country should be destroyed, yet an army of retribution would avenge us, if even no army of reinforcement could come in time to save.

The execution of the native officers was a well advised

measure, marked by all the boldness and good policy which characterised the acts of the Punjab Government. It took place on the parade in front of the church and its incongruous encirclement. Cross bars on posts had been erected, with a gun limber under each; on one flank were the 5th Native Infantry, without arms (the corps to which the culprits belonged); on the other the 4th Lancers, still armed; and between them the almost skeleton Companies of the pale faces, being a small detachment of the Company's Europeans. The men to be hung came up to the gallows with the customary indifference of their race, and climbed on to the ammunition carts. The pay havildar arranged the rope round his own neck without assistance. Their hands, I remarked, were not pinioned, as they should have been, but when the carts were removed, they did not use them as they might have done; they were resolute in dying, and one of them struggled for nearly ten minutes. Often and often have I seen natives executed, of all ages, of every caste, and every position in society, yet never have I seen one of them misbehave at the scaffold; they died with a stoicism that in Europe would excite astonishment and admiration; yet the very same men behave in some instances with the rankest cowardice in the field; crowds of them routed, and ignominiously put to flight, by merely handfuls of Europeans, few of whom, whatever their conduct in battle, would walk to execution with equal indifference.

I have heard of this difficult question in metaphysics being put to one of themselves. "It lies in the legs," he replied, "the whole fault is in the legs; often when we have made up our minds to die, and hear the cheer of the 'Goras' (pale faces), our legs carry us off against our will."

We reached Kurnaul without accident, finding there Mr. Le B———, of the Civil Service, and Captain M——

A Pandy, prior to Mutiny

—, Commissariat officer. The former amused me by his reiterated expressions of astonishment at my preferring at such a time the plains of India to Cashmere, and my freshness in the very juvenile complaint of zeal for the service. His viva voce views were faulty, but his acts were like those of almost all our countrymen when put on their mettle. He had, without escort or guard, taken up and resolutely held to an exposed post, reassuring the Zemindars by his presence, and aiding the Commissariat officer in transmitting Commissariat stores to the camp before Delhi.

I received here the Commissioner's orders, in reply to my solicitation for cancelment of leave and active employment;– a thoroughly English high-minded letter, calling me to the camp. The action of Badlee-ka-Serai had just been fought; we passed over the field the following day, eagerly anxious to reach Delhi before the storm, and nervously dreading every moment, while en route, that we should hear the salvos commence, which would declare us too late for that event which it took more than three months to bring about. Numerous dead bodies of Sepoys lay along the road by the Serai. Exposure to the sun had distended and bloated every limb; the corpse looked as though blown full of air.

We had read and heard of the murders of our women and children, so looked on with grim satisfaction on the distorted features of the dead around, limiting our pity to the case of an unfortunate pariah dog, which some stray shot had killed amidst the Sepoys, and whose body was also bloated out and distended, almost a ludicrous caricature of the human mortality around.

Speke on reaching camp went off to the tent of a friend; a hearty welcome from my Commissioner, Greathed, who was Lieutenant-Governor's agent in the

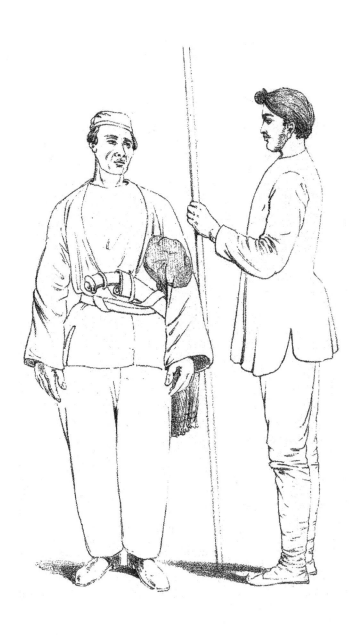

A Ghoorka Soldier of
the Sirmoor Battalion

A Young Sikh
in Undress

camp, as also from the Afghan chief, Sirdar Bahadoor, who was with him, awaited me.

Being recognised by two or three young officers on my way through the camp, they instantly proposed organising a volunteer corps of sharpshooters. This was characteristic of the men; they were on duty to the front, or on picket round the camp, constantly, but were most anxious to devote all their spare time to fighting on their own account, and I much regretted that the necessity of my entering on the duties of my proper profession, and assuming charge of the Meerut district, prevented my remaining out the operations before Delhi, and there putting to practical purpose the facility in rifle shooting which long practice as an Indian hunter had given me.

Those noble-looking fellows the Guide Corps, from the Pashawer frontier, had lately arrived, under the command of their gallant Captain Daly; his second in command, poor young Quintan Battye, lay dying of a mortal wound at the time. The regiment was called out during the afternoon to repel an attack from the city. They were a powerful looking and admirably equipped body of men, dressed entirely in dust-coloured clothing, excepting the turbans, which were a dark indigo. A Ressaldar of these men I heard, on that day, had a single combat with a native officer of the 3rd Light Cavalry, when riding out on the plain, between the ridge on which our camp was pitched and the city. The Ressaldar, a Mussulman Wulytee, or Afghan, went forward to meet his rival of the rebel host. Asiatics never thrust with their swords, but after a few rapid cuts and guards, the head of the mutineer regular was swept from his body, and the Guide seizing the bridle of the dead man's horse, a powerful stud bred, plundered by its late owner from Government, and springing into the saddle, turned to his men, as he lifted his dripping sword over his head, and exclaimed, "Allah-u-Akbar! and by the blessing of the Prophet, may we all get mounted in a similar manner."

In the frontispiece of this sketch I have placed a likeness of one of the Sirmoor Battalion of Ghoorkas who were then in camp. The jealousy of enlistment for our army shown by the Nepaulese Government, who are naturally desirous of keeping as many as possible of the real Ghoorkalee for their own regiments, renders recruiting from that class difficult, and Hill Rajpoots or Coolies are often taken into our Hill corps. The Ghoorkas of the Sirmoor Battalion, however, appear to be a corps of picked men even amongst their own countrymen. I doubt if Jung Bahadoor himself could show a body of more active, robust, and reckless soldiers than those chimpanzee-faced little *enfans perdus*, who held the right of our position in company with their admirably disciplined representatives in our own army – the 60th Royal Rifles.

The fraternisation and *entente cordiale* between Reid's little Sirmoories and Jones' Royals were most complete, and, in many instances, comical. They shared their grog, and walked about arm-in-arm, interchanging sentiments on the world at large in a compound dialect of Oordoo mixed with Nagree and Sanscrit phrases, and British, mixed with a good deal of the barrack-room classics, which despise the use of euphonisms. The pains and attention bestowed by the riflemen in imparting a smattering of the English language to their little Ghoorka companions, would, if their choice of easy lessons for beginners had been more discreet, have entitled them to the thanks of our Minister of Instruction. The phrases imparted were, however, owing perhaps to the locality of the school, so heavily double-shotted that it is impossible to print even a specimen.

27

The Ghoorkas are said to have expressed great indignation at a report, once current in the camp, of their being removed from their dangerous position at Hindoo Rao's house. They had a right, they considered, to be posted with their "Bhais" (brothers), the English riflemen. They were therefore with them throughout, shared in their honours and dangers, and finally, when the 60th left for Meerut, their little pupils turned out to bid them farewell, presenting arms to them when they marched away.

By "Ghoorkas," I mean the class usually called so by Anglo-Indians. They are not the real Ghoorka, however, but much superior to them in strength, activity, and courage: they are very short, Tartar-featured, of great muscular development, and come chiefly from the district of Nuggur in Nepaul. The real Ghoorkas, of whom Jung Bahadoor and his brothers are specimens, have regular and handsome features, in no respect resembling those daredevil monkey-faced little soldiers, who at Delhi made the name of the Sirmoorees so honoured.

I give from characteristic sketches by my talented friend, H.G.K., specimens of the classes of natives who have been the principal actors in the present war. The first two may be considered the polished results of our own patient instruction and political fatuity; the last are the raw material from which Sir John Lawrence raised the means of saving India.

Greathed, the Commissioner, intimated to me on the day of my arrival in camp, that as my *locum tenens* at Meerut was killed, and it was of great importance that some one with local experience should be in charge of the Meerut district, I must find my way across as soon as possible, but that owing to the scarcity of cavalry I could not have an escort allowed me. I determined to start the same night, having hired a horse belonging to one of the Kut-cherrie Sowars, or mounted messengers, with the Commissioner, and taking four of the same class belonging to my own district, whom I found in camp with me. Our bugles sounding the alarm just before I started, caused a delay till midnight in my departure. I then, however, slipped out of the camp, carrying dispatches from the Commissioner, and, giving the parole to the last of our videttes, set my course for Bhagput on the Jumna, *en route* for Meerut, without any opportunity of bidding adieu to poor Speke, whom I never saw again.

Having been up for three days and nights consecutively, I reached Bhagput overcome with fatigue. The native officials, Kurrum Ali, Tehsildar, and Wuzeer Khan, Thannadar, appeared delighted to see me, and accepted the possibility of Sahib's riding about the country as a sign of returning security. They vied with each other in offering me hospitality. The first is now a proved staunch servant of Government; the latter a prisoner in chains in the Meerut gaol, for traitorous correspondence with Delhi.

I had thrown myself down and gone to sleep, on arriving at Bhagput, and on awaking I found a crowd of natives, chiefly Rajpoots and Bunyahs, around me. The Mussulmans of Bhagput were then ripe for rebellion.

An attack on the Bridge of Boats by the rebel Sah Mull and his Goojurs was daily expected; and I devoted a portion of the night to reporting matters to the Commissioner, soliciting the detachment of a force to protect the bridge and keep open the communication with Meerut, and advising the Rajpoots as to a plan of defence for the town. A force was sent from the Delhi Camp, which failed lamentably in its duty; but the resistance of the townsmen was of some use against their Goojur assailants.

I was unable to ride during the heat of the day, but reached Meerut the next night, and found great difficulty in passing the numberless trenches and guards surrounding the station. Carefully eschewing the Dum Dumma, as the entrenched position was called, the very atmosphere of which appeared to have a depressing influence on its inhabitants, I took up my residence in a house in cantonments, where I found Major W———, the only European, apparently, who thought a parapet and ditch around him unnecessary. He proved a useful agent afterwards; and I shall have frequent mention to make of him. I will now recall the various incidents prior to, or during the Meerut outbreak, up to the date of my return.

Chapter Three

The commencement of the year 1857 brought with it to Meerut, as elsewhere, the first mutterings of that storm which was so soon to burst over our Indian Empire, but its warnings at Meerut, as elsewhere, were unheeded.

Individuals indeed quoted, as I have frequently myself heard, the memorable prophecy of Sir Charles Metcalfe, who when passing a Sepoy in English accoutrements and arms, exclaimed to a friend, "There goes one of the greatest enemies of our British power in the East."

We have ourselves heard animated discussions arise from even a distant allusion to the want of a stern discipline for the Sepoy army, some latent suspicion of the false foundations of their position rendering only more jealous of challenge those gallant but mistaken English officers whose false *esprit de corps* has since led to such fatal results for themselves.

In the end of February and beginning of March, several of the village watchmen reported at the police stations, that they had duly carried out the verbal instructions conveyed to them by the watchmen of the eastward villages, and transmitted copies of certain little cakes received from them.

The village watchmen erroneously supposed that these cakes were distributed by order of Government. Their course was traced back from this to the Allyghur district. The watchman of a neighbouring village generally ran into the next with a cake the size of a crown piece in his hand, and intimated to his *confrère* that "the orders were" that he should make two, four, or more similar ones and deliver them at once at any village where they had not been received, repeating this order to each. The message, meaningless as it appeared, travelled throughout the country with great rapidity.

The transmission of such little cakes from one district to another is supposed by the Hindoos to effect the removal of epidemic disease. When cholera broke out in this division, the villagers frequently attached the disease, as they fancied, by some ceremonies to a buffalo, and drove it across the Ganges or into some other village. This latter course frequently caused fighting between the villagers.

It was also found that a similar transmission of cakes had taken place on a former occasion, when a murrain attacked the cattle of the districts bordering Oude, and the disease was supposed to be stayed as soon as the said cakes reached the holy fanes of Hurdwar. The agitation was fostered, and false rumours founded thereon, prejudicial to Government, were almost invariably propagated by Mussulmans, while the transmission of a cake is a purely Hindoo practice. The shape and size of the cakes was that of the common Brahmin "Pooree."

The excitement at the time among the Sepoys, and the occurrence afterwards of the mutiny, has led many to connect this cake distribution with our disturbances, but without any sufficient grounds for so doing. It is probable that if any connexion existed it was accidental, and the relationship acknowledged by either designing or ignorant persons was consequent upon the distribution, and did not cause or precede it.

Those, indeed, who have attempted to explain the "Chupatee movement," as it is called, to be a sort of "fiery cross " signal for a united rising, appear to have succeeded in proving little by their own ingenuity. Its real origin was, doubtless, a superstitious attempt to prevent any return of the fearful visitation of epidemic cholera which devastated the North-West Provinces the year before, and still lingered in scattered spots.

The readiness with which facts, in themselves insignificant, are invested with importance at such a time, may be judged of also by the romance founded on the appearance of a certain faqueer at a large tank near Meerut, called the "Suruj khoond." He encamped there with several followers on an elephant, and was warned off by the officiating magistrate. It was reported, as soon as the mutinies broke out, that he was one of the Princes of Delhi in disguise, whose mission from the King had been to tamper with the soldiery. Great regret was afterwards expressed that this man had not been seized, but the inquiries since made by Major Williams, Superintendent of Cantonment Police, tend to prove that the man was a Sikh faqueer from the Punjab.

On the 23d April, the skirmishers of the 3d Light Cavalry, ninety in number, paraded to learn a new mode of breaking cartridges and loading. All but five men refused to receive the cartridges at all, though they were the same they had been in the habit of using, intimating that they would be disgraced in the eyes of the other regiments if they did so. The recusants were tried by court-martial, and sentenced, some to ten, others to five years' imprisonment each for mutiny, and made over for imprisonment to Mr. Johnston, officiating District Officer at the time.

Considerable excitement prevailed in the city and district; the Sepoys were ripe for revolt, and an outbreak of some kind was by many deemed imminent. No preventive

A Mussulman Irregular Sowar, (Mutineer)

measures were taken, however, and on Sunday evening, the 10th May, when the Rifles and other English troops were parading for church, a cook-boy, running down to the lines of the 20th, and other native troops, called out to them that the Europeans were being got ready to disarm them; and a Sowar of the 3rd Cavalry, riding up to the men of the Sepoy companies, asked them what they waited for – the English troops were coming. This instantly fanned the smouldering fire to flame. The Sepoys flew to their bells of arms, loaded their muskets, and shot down the officers who attempted to remonstrate with them, while the Sowars of the 3d Cavalry, riding about the Station, cut down every European they met.

Most of the respectable portion of the native inhabitants shut themselves up in their houses, but the swarms of armed ruffians, with which every Indian city is infested, commenced burning and plundering all the bungalow near the lines and city with a rapidity and facility which might have led a stranger to suppose them familiar with and practiced at the work.

The Mussulman Budmashes of the Cantonment Bazar were the leaders in the work of destruction, and the most brutal murder committed – that of an officer's wife, whose clothes were set on fire – was afterwards proved against a Mussulman butcher, who was hanged for the crime.

The outbreak commenced at the time of evening church parade, about 6 p.m., and for some time the military authorities appear to have been paralysed. The Carabineers and guns, when they were marched down to the native lines, were taken by the most circuitous route, so that for about two hours, when every moment perilled life, the native cantonments were in the hands of an armed mob. Her Majesty's 60th Rifles, a corps whose light infantry organisation eminently qualified them for dealing with such a crisis, were not employed at all in clearing out the quarter where they were most required; and finally, when the tumult was over, and the mutineers, broken and disorganised, were hurrying from the station in small parties, when natural probabilities and common sense caused numbers of the officers present to exclaim – "They are off to Delhi," no attempt at pursuit was made, – no effort to save our countrymen and countrywomen from the massacre which would inevitably follow the advent of the mutineers to a station with only native troops in it.

Most of the mutineers went off by the direct trunk road to Delhi, burning and plundering the Tehsil of Moradnugger on their way. Some also went by the Bhagput route; but all were in broken and detached parties, which might readily have been cut off in detail by cavalry and artillery.

The military authorities appear to have overrated to a ridiculous extent the amount of danger to be apprehended from the men of the city and the villages. The following remarks by Mr. W. H. Carey, of Roorkee, represent opinions very generally held at this time throughout the country:–

"All the subsequent dreadful bloodshed and loss of human life in so many stations, might never have occurred, had the mutineers from Meerut been prevented reaching Delhi, as they could easily have been. It is a notorious fact that the 60th Rifles were assembled, ready to move on the evening of the disturbance fully half an hour before they received the order to move, and then, when they did receive the order, they were marched at funeral pace the whole way, instead of going at a 'double quick.' Arrived at the scene of operations, the brave fellows, burning with vengeance, and ready to rush on and exterminate the rascally natives, were to their intense disgust made little more than mere spectators of what was going on. Natives were rushing about on all sides, yelling, plundering, burning and murdering, and yet the troops were for a long time not allowed to fire upon them nor apprehend them. The men were then marched back to the Mall, and there bivouacked, leaving more than half of the station to the mercy of the spoliators. The native regiments, after doing all the damage they could, marched off in triumph to Delhi. They were not even pursued to the cantonment boundaries. We had two magnificent European regiments at Meerut struggling and straining in the slips, but the dogs of war were not let loose. The route the mutineers had taken was at once conjectured, and it was also self-evident that every European at Delhi would be attacked and slaughtered. Yet no attempt at rescue was made. No wonder the Delhi Sepoy at once joined them, when they saw all that a handful of men had been able to do, in the face of the finest European Brigade in India. No wonder that Delhi became a perfect hive for the discontented and mutinous."

The following account of the mutiny was written by Gungapershad, Tehsildar of Meerut. I give it in his own words. He had received an English education at the Government College of Bareilly; and, like the great majority of those natives who have been taught the English language, and acquired the information inseparable from so doing, he has been true and loyal throughout.

"In the end of April some of the 3d Cavalry Barracks were set on fire, and every second or third night something similar happened. Every one believed the troops were to mutiny. On the 8th of May, when eighty-five Sowars were sentenced and confined in gaol, mutiny was expected, but nothing occurred that day. On Sunday, the 10th of May, 1857, about 5p.m., while I was disposing of some cases in the Tehsil, my guard Peon told me the Bunyahs of the Sudder were coming, and hurriedly talking of the regiments mutinying against their officers; but I would not believe them. Again they told me firing was distinctly heard; on which I came out, and saw a multitude of people coming from the Sudder into the city, who, when asked, repeated what I had heard before.

I dismissed the office, and taking my sword and rifle stood at the gate, as also did the few Tehsil Peons who were present on the spot.

"A 3d Cavalry trooper was seen proceeding at full gallop towards the new gaol. He was heard saying, 'Brothers! Hindoos and Mussulmans! Make haste to join with us in the religious war to which we are going.' Then another followed, and in a very short interval some fifty passed, all going towards the new gaol, and a good number of Sepoys accompanied them. About sunset I heard they broke the gaol, and got their brethren released.

"I was soon surprised to see hundreds coming from the Sudder, amongst whom I saw a good many who were not Sepoys, shouting 'Ali! Ali!' They rushed into the house formerly occupied by Mr. Blunt, and then into the Civil Court, both of which they looted and set on fire.

The other band of mutineers, accompanied with gaol Nujeebs and other Budmashes, returned after breaking the gaol and joined with those in the Civil Court. "First, two of the 3d Cavalry Sowars advanced towards the Tehsil, and inquired where I, the Tehsildar, was, and on being pointed out, they threatened me, and demanded the delivery of the keys of the Treasury, which I refused, when they advanced with drawn swords towards me. I shot one of them with my rifle, and loading again from behind the wall, I also shot the other. When their comrades saw them falling, the whole gang, some hundreds, rushed in, shouting 'Ali! Ali!' and 'Naré Hyduree!' with drawn swords and muskets, and then I saw resistance was of no use, and everyone ready to kill me. I jumped down the Tehsil wall, and, taking flight, concealed myself in the house of a native gentleman. Here I heard they looted the Tehsil Treasury, and my house and the Tehsil; burnt my English books, maps, property and instruments, and all Government records and papers, the Commissioner's (the late Mr. Greathed's) house, the Civil Court, and in fact all the adjoining public buildings; and that the looted property was without any fear bought by the city Budmashes, and that the villagers bad also come down to plunder the lines and cantonments. I also heard that the Mussulmans and Pulladars of the Bazar, and the butchers, were murdering Europeans and the few Christian pensioners who reside in Smith Gunge, but nobody mentioned any particular names, and the cry of 'Ali! Ali!' lasted till midnight, when I heard the mutineers had all left for Delhi. Unfounded and false reports were current all night.

Here is a list of the Europeans murdered at Meerut on the night of the 10th May, 1857:—

3d Light Cavalry.

Lieutenant C. I. E. Mc Nabb, Veterinary Surgeon Philips, and Veterinary Surgeon Dawson.

11th Regiment N. I.

Lieutenant-Colonel J. Finnis.

20th Regiment N. I.

Captain J. H. Taylor, Captain D. McDonald, Lieutenant D. Henderson, and Lieutenant W. Pattle.

Mrs. Captain McDonald, Mrs. Captain Chambers, Mrs. Dawson and two children, Mrs. Courtenay and two children, Mr. V. Tregear, Pensioners McKinley and Blanco, Corporals Mortimer (Rifles), Edwardes, and Fitzpatrick, and wives, Mr. Newland (Photographer), Overseers Sergeants Law and two children, McPhee, Binglee, Grant, Brooks, and wives, Gunners Donohoe. Conolly, Benson and Cairns (Horse Artillery), Riding Master Langdale's child.

At one spot, in the burying-ground of Meerut, lie grouped together the victims of the mutiny, a small headstone or tablet recording simply the name and date of death of each. Within the same graveyard, and at a short distance off, lie two heroes of the olden days, well known to fame, – Sir David Ochterlony, the conqueror of our Hill provinces, and General Gillespie, the hero of Kalunga, a Ghoorka fort in the Dehra Dhoon.

Chapter Four

One of the first acts of the mutineers had been to release their comrades confined in the new gaol between the Civil lines and the Suruj Khoond, while the rioters and gaol guard set free all the other prisoners, both of the old and new gaols, amounting at that time to nearly 1800. Numbers of villagers came into the station even on the first night to plunder, and this number increased much during the two following nights; many of the prisoners released had enemies in the district, mostly Bunyahs who had brought suits in our courts, and the arrival of a period of anarchy was at once seized on by them to wreak a summary revenge on almost all the Bunyah caste. Thus at the village of Bhojpore, the best house, a large brick building with a courtyard in the centre and massive wooden portals, belonged to the family of a Mahajun or Bunyah, by name Beharee Lall, who was a 4 Biswa (or one-fifth) sharer of that village; one of the other shareholders, a Jât, was at the time of the outbreak in prison, confined for debt under Civil court decree at the suit of the Bunyah. He arrived during the night of the 11th at Bhojpore with a few of his fellow prisoners, and at daylight the villagers were collected for an attack on the Bunyah's house. The gross cowardice or the helpless apathy of these Bunyahs is proverbial.

It is a common saying among the natives, that a Bunyah being found possessed of personal courage, is a sure sign of illegitimacy. The Bunyahs of Bhojpore merely barred the door, and while it was being cut through with axes remained huddled together in the court of their house nerveless, and, on an entry being effected, of the eight men there assembled seven were cut to pieces; one only survived, though he too had received seven sword wounds and was left for dead. The gentle Hindoo or the Indianized Mussulman, while he tortures and destroys his victim, is as selfishly and absolutely free of all feeling for his anguish as the jaw of the shark or the alligator for the living prey it crushes. The sole survivor's account, however, led to the arrest afterwards of most of the parties concerned, six of whom were executed, and many imprisoned for various terms.

Most of the troops were under arms during the night of the 10th; but on the next day, the European and Eurasian inhabitants generally entered the field magazine enclosure, a space about two hundred yards square, surrounded by a brick wall eight feet high. A trench was rapidly dug round this wall, the earth from the ditch being thrown up against it, and, with bastions at the corners, this formed the "Dum Dumma," as the natives call it, which held a prominent place in our local history for the next six months.

On the morning of the 12th, the first of the Delhi refugees arrived, bringing the account of the massacre at that station; during that, and for some following days, ladies, gentlemen, and even young girls, for whom an hour's exposure to the sun at such a season would have been deemed dangerous, arrived, after wandering about for days among the villages on the road. Some of the villagers behaved with kindness to the refugees. Cases were, however, common in which their helplessness called down insult upon them.

The only tribe which made itself conspicuous for its cruelty in robbing and threatening them, were the Goojurs. These men, a sect of Hindoos located only in the neighbourhood of the Meerut district, have long been noted as inveterate robbers. They are cattle-stealers by profession, and, like most of the predatory tribes, take employment (whenever they find officials foolish enough to trust them with it) as watchmen, or village police. These men, at the first commencement of the outbreak, rose throughout the district, rendered many of the roads even near Meerut dangerous or impassable, and in the lowlands on the bank of the Ganges they robbed and plundered indiscriminately, whenever they found any weaker than themselves; but they have nevertheless no ill-will against the English Government. They plundered the mutineers as readily as the Europeans, if found in as defenceless a condition; and they completely gutted the temple of Parushnath at Hustnapore. They have now made common cause with the rebels of Bijnour, merely because the latter give them better promise of indulgence in their passion for plunder. The sad history, indeed, of the anarchy lately existing in the Meerut "Khadir," is written in the whitening skulls and skeletons of numberless travellers now bleaching by the jungle paths of Hustnapore.

Among those who failed in their escape from Delhi to Meerut, was the party with whom was Lieutenant Willoughby, the hero of the Delhi magazine. The duty of investigating the particulars of this young officer's death, fell to the writer of this sketch, as District Officer. I visited the spot just after the fall of Delhi, and made the following notes on the subject.

Lieutenant Willoughby, of the Artillery (one of the heroes of the Delhi magazine), Lieutenant Butler, and Lieutenant Angelo, both of the 54th N.I., Lieutenant Hyslop, a Mr. Stewart, of the Delhi College, and a sixth (name unknown), left Delhi with Lieutenant Osborne, of the 54th N. I., on the 11th of May, and got to the village of Negpore, on the bank of the Hindun, where they were well treated, fed, and sheltered in a grove near a village. Lieutenant Osborne had been wounded in Delhi by a musket-ball through the thigh; and when the rest of the party went on to Koomhera, he found himself unable to accompany them. He eventually, however, reached Dhoubree, whence he was sent into Meerut by Syud Ashruff Ali.

Lieutenant Willoughby's party, when near the village of Koomhera, were required by one Kâna, an Acharuj Brahmin, a resident of the village, to make them a present. Their only weapons appear to have been a carbine, for which they had no bullets, and one or two regulation swords. They represented to the footpad, who addressed them, that they had fallen into misfortune, and that the only means of defence left to them in their distress were these weapons, which they refused to part with, telling Kâna to go on his way, and they would go on theirs. What further may have passed, I have no account of Kâna's object was to get the carbine, and it ended in one of the officers (probably Lieutenant Willoughby, who carried it), shooting him through the chest with a copper Mussooree pice. He called out for assistance, and as the cry was passed on, the inhabitants of five villages turned out, so as to enclose the party of fugitives.

These villages were;

Koomhera ....Acharuj and Tugga
                            Brahmins.
Bunnuhra ....Tugga Brahmins.
Giaspore................Tugga Brahmins.

Sohana....................Tugga Brahmins.

Kundoura...............Tugga Brahmins.

Three of the party were killed close to Koomhera; the others got away a short distance to the side of a canal cut, where they also were killed.

Lieutenant Willoughby and party appear to have been sacrificed to one of those prejudices which the natives know right well how to parade under encouragement, or to forget altogether if expedient. The deceased Kâna was a Brahmin, and the comparative defencelessness of the Europeans, with the overwhelming numbers of their assailants, alike doomed the whole party to destruction for the death of one of the holy caste. I could find no exculpatory circumstances in the conduct of any one of the Brahmins of Koomhera: no attempt to save or assist any of the officers while being murdered appears to have been made.

All the inhabitants of villages having murder or rebellion to account for, generally make a point of leaving their houses empty so long as any strong force of police may be in the neighbourhood. I ascertained that this was the case with the villages above alluded to, and therefore passed on to Moradnugger from Ratoul, visiting Koomhera by a return march from the latter place; and, surrounding it at night, we found five Brahmins, besides an aged Kahar, a Bunyah, and some women and children: these last we removed prior to burning and destroying the village. The grain and other property was taken into Moradnugger and sold for Government. The five Brahmins I hanged the same evening.

Owing to the entire destruction of Lieutenant

A Goorka Soldier   *A Sikh Servant Of Rajahlal Sing*

Willoughby's party, it will probably never be accurately ascertained who struck the numerous blows by which they were murdered, but a number of the chief men of the villages which were concerned in the offense have since been arrested and are under trial.

Syud Ashruff Ali, who saved the life of Lieutenant Osborne, has been put in possession of one or two villages formerly owned by Willoughby's murderers, and the Mussulman cultivators who hospitably fed, so far as their humble means permitted, the entire party afterwards killed, have been recommended to Government for a reward of one thousand rupees each, and a number of the chief men of the villages above named as concerned in the murder have since been arrested by our police, and are now under trial.

The act of Lieutenant Willoughby above alluded to, has since frequently been commented on in very unjust terms, on the plea that submission to the demand might have saved the lives of the party. There is much, however, to admire in that stern courage which knew no dread of numbers. Had Willoughby been a man to surrender his arms to villagers, he never could have blown up the Delhi magazine.

About the 12th May news arrived at the station of the rising of the Rajpoots and Rughurs near Sirdhanah. The chief of the Rajpoots, however, Rhydul of Rarhduna, forwarded timely information to the Tehsildar that he would soon be attacked by one Nurput Sing, of Ukulpoora, at the head of a large body of men. The Tehsildar made his preparations, got out the Treasury guard, consisting of the twelve police Nujeebs armed with muskets, and drove off his assailants with a loss of fifteen of their number killed. They, however, plundered the bazaar, and for some time levied a daily fine from the residents of

Sirdhanah. The nuns of the Sirdhanah convent were escorted into Meerut by a party of volunteers, headed by the Postmaster, Mr. Moore, no regular troops being "available" for the duty.

At this time Sah Mul, a Mâvee Jhat, zemindar of Bijroal, performed his first act of open defiance of authority, by attacking and plundering a large party of Brinjara merchants.

He next attacked and burnt the Tehsil of Burout, and shortly after obtained the appointment of soubadar of that Pergunnah from the titular king of Delhi. The conduct of Kurum Alli Khan, Tehsildar of Burout, a Mussulman native of the Rohtuck district, is deserving of notice; he having, with the assistance of Nawul Sing, a Rajpoot zemindar of Deola, carried off a large amount of Government revenue lying in the Tehsil treasury at the time. Mushroom dignities could of course spring up in a night while society was so unhinged; and a Havildar who had been sent to the Binoulee Pergunnah, to purchase some 1600 rupees' worth of blankets for his regiment, followed Sah Mul's example, by appropriating the money, and proclaiming himself "king" in Nirpoora.

Mr. Johnston finding it necessary to inflict some punishment on the Goojur village of Ikhteyarpore, obtained the help of a small escort of Carbineers, and rode out to that village.

The Goojurs, conscious of many a raid not strictly justifiable by any but their own code of law, had disappeared from the place; but the grass roofs of their huts were burnt, and the party set out on their return to Meerut, which was only about ten miles off. As poor Johnston was cantering on in advance, his horse fell and fractured his rider's skull. Of this mortal injury Mr.

Johnston died on the 27th May. Government lost by his death one of the most hard-working, serviceable, and valuable of their servants; one of the many plodding, high principled, and thoroughly trained men, whose labours have done much to impress the people of the country with the thorough honesty of our intentions, and our anxiety, despite the difficulty of an unlimited amount of work to be performed, and a very limited agency for its performance, to be strictly just to all.

Mr. Johnston's place was filled for about a fortnight by Mr. T———, ex-collector of Boolundshehur, whose attempt to punish the Goojurs of Gagoul, and burn their village, was partially frustrated by the treachery of the Kotwal of Meerut, Rao Kishen Sing, a relative of their afterwards famous Toola Ram of Rewaree, and who, after flying from Mr. T———'s indignation at Meerut, was killed, fighting against us, on the battle-field of Narnoul.

Urgent requisitions for assistance came in from the neighbouring district of Boolundshehur, to the military authorities, both in May and June. There were at the time of the outbreak about three lacs of rupees in that treasury, then guarded by a detachment of the 9th Native Infantry. A very small party, even fifty riflemen, might with facility have gone out and escorted that treasure with safety into Meerut. So infatuated do the authorities appear to have been, that to every remonstrance of the district officer, Mr. S———, the invariable reply of "not a man can be spared," was returned.

On the 29th May, however, a column of troops under Colonel, now Sir Archdale Wilson, left the cantonments for Delhi, and soon after won those first fruits of victory, that earnest of after successes, the details of which belong to other records.

A Sikh Recruit.   *A Mussulmam Sowar.*

Chapter Five

About the 15th of June, nine Sikh horsemen without arms rode up to my house, and reported their advent to me as district officer. They had just come up country from a detachment of the 1st Oude Cavalry, which had mutinied. They had seen Captain Hayes cut down by his faithful followers, while raising a glass of water to his lips; had seen Captain Barber and another officer killed, and had left their companions en route for Delhi. They had surrendered their arms to Mr. Watson, magistrate of Allyghur, and now came to seek employment under Government. Their names were as follows:– Juggut Sing, Jowala Sing, Lall Sing, Boodh Sing, Nahal Sing, Surroop Sing, Mehtab Sing, Tummun Sing, Paka Sing.

The term "Sing or Lion" is adopted by all Sikhs, and the sketch which accompanies this work shows the characteristic appearance of these men. I was delighted to get them, and right good service these gallant fellows did in many an after foray.

Almost immediately after their arrival, Mr. W—, of Moradabad, who had long been exerting himself at that station to keep the 29th Native Infantry staunch, proposed that one of the Sikhs should accompany a faithful Mussulman Sowar of his to meet the mutineers of the Bareilly brigade, then at Gujrowla, across the Ganges, and detach if possible the Sikh companies from them. Poor Tummun Sing went off with his Sowar, whose name was, I believe, Nusseer Khan, of the 8th Irregulars, and the result was afterwards described to us by a Beldar, or

Coolie, who accompanied them. The Sikh was disguised as a Faqueer; of course without arms. The vanguard of the troops which they met consisted of Sowars of the 8th Irregulars, to whom the Mussulman going up abruptly, announced that his companion was a Sikh spy, sent to corrupt the 29th Native Infantry, and Tummun Sing was, as a matter of course, immediately cut to pieces; the faithful Mahomedan accompanying his co-religionists to Delhi. All the rest of the Sikh party are now officers, four being jemadars, and four duffadars, for services during the disturbances.

The residents of the station at Boolundshehur had then been driven out by Wulee Dad Khan, the rebel chief of Malaghur. Young Lieutenant T———, and Mr. L———, of the Civil Service, with a small body of Irregular Horse, who might daily be expected to mutiny, and cut their throats, gallantly held the village of Haupper on the Grand Trunk Road. News arriving that Wulee Dad Khan threatened that place from Galowtee, an expedition consisting of Carbineers and Rifles, with two Horse Artillery guns, were sent against him.

I accompanied the force as a volunteer. We marched all night, having thirty-five miles to go before we reached Galowtee, where a few footmen were overtaken and killed; but the main body of the rebels had fled. The Jâts of Bethownah, however, turned out to assist the British troops, being sworn foes to Wulee Dad Khan and his allies, the Goojurs; three of whose villages they sacked and burnt, killing fifteen of the inhabitants just as we were leaving the place. By the time we got back to Haupper, or rather Babooljhur, in its neighbourhood, we had marched upwards of fifty miles; we were out till late in the day, and the heat was excessive. Two of the Carbineers who, by some regimental folly, were compelled to wear brass helmets, got a stroke of the sun; and three horses died during the afternoon and following night, of fatigue. A considerable party of us slept in the house of Charles D'O——, of the Stud Department. It was then filled with all the comforts and luxuries of Indian life, in way of sofas, arm-chairs, silver and china ornaments, &c. &c, which might all before then have been easily removed to Meerut, but the precaution would have shown a dread of what all thought would happen.

Englishmen appear, in some instances, blessed with an almost Turkish fatalism; and all the property was, a few days later, totally destroyed by the Bareilly brigade. During the night an express from the Ganges Ghaut at Ghurmukhtesar, brought us the news that the Bareilly mutineers were then about to cross the river. T—— and D'O—— went off to try and persuade the officer commanding the detachment to march to the Ghaut and oppose the crossing; his orders, however, allowed him no discretion.

As soon, therefore, as I could get to Meerut, representing the political necessities of the case, and the lamentable effect on the district, of allowing these men a triumphal progress across the Doab, I tried to rouse the worthy old general to letting us go down with a couple of hundred men and two guns to the Ghaut. He replied by calling a council of war, which, of course, "did not fight." The public shortly afterwards approved the orders of the officer commanding-in-chief, who granted six months' leave to the Hills to our general; but I may mention, that the said public gave the old general blame for numberless omissions and commissions, especially on the night of the outbreak, not justly attributable to him.

I think now, as I thought then, that we could have driven, the enemy, though about 2,500, from the Ghaut;

but even had we failed, our lives would have been well expended. It was advisable, in so early a stage of the struggle, to show these men what Englishmen could dare to do; and it must be remembered that the assault of Delhi, which was arranged for the night of the day on which the Bareilly brigade marched over the Jumna Bridge, with their Christian bandsmen playing "Cheer, boys, cheer," was postponed for months by their arrival. How many lives might have been saved,– what months of protracted disturbances might not have been prevented, had we delayed the Bareilly brigade even for a day.

When I received charge of the Meerut District, no revenue had been collected since the outbreak. It was, of course, impossible to get remittances of treasure. The Mahajuns and Bunyahs of the city, with the characteristic generosity of their race, refused to advance a loan to Government as a return for one hundred years of fostering care. The Company's copper coinage, which would not, like silver, pass current under a native government, was sold at a heavy discount in the bazaar. Our Meerut treasure, which amounted to about five lacs when the outbreak commenced, dwindled down by necessary expenditure on fortifications, Commissariat supplies, pay of troops, &c. &c, to less than one. Military aid for revenue collections could not be counted on; but the ready co-operation and invaluable assistance of Colonel W———, the brigade-major, enabled me to effect all that was necessary, by organising a volunteer troop of the European civil, and other officers, then refugees in Meerut. Colonel W———had promised me his aid in getting horses, arms, and accoutrements for a dozen yeomanry if necessary.

The first attempt to raise that comparatively trifling number, under one of my acting assistants, had failed; but, counting on the ever-ready help of my friend the brigade-major, for arming all who could be procured, I entered on the duty of recruiting-sergeant for a body of volunteers, to be called, after Daly's gallant horsemen, The Guides, whom I had seen in Delhi, "The Khakee Ressalah;" their dress being a complete dust-coloured suit, which gave them a most sombre but workman like appearance. The first score of names I collected by personally soliciting accession to the ranks; and as no programme of rules for the regulation of volunteer corps had, up to that time, reached Meerut, I got the troopers who first volunteered to sign a paper, promising to parade for duty whenever called upon, and to obey the orders of my friend Major W———, Superintendent of Police, on whose zealous co-operation I could depend, and whose name I entered as commanding officer, without consulting.

On his accepting the post, and obtaining the aid of D'O——— and T———, as second in command and adjutant, those I had enlisted were called together. Many others volunteered, and so actively was the drilling, mounting, arming, &c. Sic, proceeded with by our adjutant, that within three days a troop of Englishman, Eurasians, and a few Sikhs, was fit for duty. The political aspect of the district at the time, and the objects with which the volunteer horsemen were embodied, are detailed in the following memorandum, furnished by me to the General of Division, when requesting his aid.

"The Goojurs throughout this district are in open rebellion, and, either with or without his consent, have elected Kuddum Sing, of Purreechutghur, Rajah of the Eastern Pergunnah of Meerut. The police have been driven out of Purreechutghur, and report that Kuddum Sing has there dug up three guns which were concealed underground, and mounted them on his fort, in furtherance of the plan of establishing a Goojur

Government. The Goojurs of Booklana, Himmutpore, and a number of places in the vicinity of Purreechutghur, have attacked and plundered the well-affected Jât villages, burning their houses, and butchering the inhabitants. Kuddum Sing can command some 10,000 men.

"The Zemindar of Bajrool, Sah Mull, *alias* Maho Sing, having plundered the town and Tehsil of Barout, having plundered the bazaar of Bhagput, and broken the bridge, has now at his command some 5,000 ruffians, nearly all Goojurs, of whom the most dangerous are 200 escaped prisoners of the Meerut gaol. Sah Mull is now reported to be about to destroy the bridge over the Hindun, which would, during the rains, interfere materially with our communications with head-quarters.*

"The Goojurs, accustomed, many of them, to a life of robbing and danger, and assembling in thousands under regular leaders, who act without scruple in defiance of Government, are more than a match for our Jât friends.

* *The Goojurs are numerous in the North-West Provinces: they are to be found about Sirsa Rewarrie, Delhi, Meerut, and Allygurh, as also in the northern parts of Bondeylkund; the Raja of Sumptur being of their clan.*

Colonel Tod, and other authorities, have considered them to be derived from the Aborigines of India; they themselves claim to be descended from Rajput fathers and mothers of inferior castes. Their former importance may be gathered from the fact, that they gave the name to Guzerat, in Western India, and to Goojerat, in the Punjab. Some parts of Seharunpur, too, were in the last century called, after them, Guzerat.

The Goojurs are all at heart plunderers and cattle stealers; and though compelled to give up their roving habits, and taking to agriculture to some extent, yet it will be seen that during the disturbances they have not failed to return to other and more congenial pursuits.

In the days of Thuggie the Goojurs originated and practiced a distinct branch of the calling, viz. the "Megh punnah," or murdering the parents and male children, but preserving the females for the purpose of supplying the harems of the Mahommetans at Delhi.

Scattered over a large territory, and without recognised chiefs, the Jâts have almost invariably behaved nobly in the support of law and order; Junnaiyut Sing and Ruttun Sing having especially distinguished themselves in the service of Lieutenant Tyrwhitt, at Babooljhur."

"The Rajpoots at Deolah under Nawul Sing are most anxious to be organized for the Government service; all the friends of Government throughout the district complain that their hands are tied while our enemies are free to act as they list. It will be the duty of the Meerut Volunteer Horse to raise the friends of Government throughout the district, to assist and encourage them in fighting our sworn enemies the rebel Goojurs, and in punishing such villages and bands of Dacoits as can be disposed of without regular troops.

"It will also be the duty of the Volunteers to assist in keeping open the communication between this station and the neighbouring ones; in fact, undertaking, either within the district or beyond it, such duties as their limited numbers can perform."

"In consequence of the district being at present left totally unprotected, it has become almost totally unprotected, it has become almost totally disorganised; wholesale butcheries and plunderings are prevalent throughout it, and, unless some vigorous measures are taken to assist our friends and punish our foes, we shall be totally deserted by the mass of the people, those still faithful to us are becoming disgusted at our apparent apathy, and the mutiny and rebellion of to-day may become a revolution."

Few of those who so gallantly volunteered for a life of peril and adventure in lieu of patient anticipation, while awaiting the issue of the struggle at Delhi, had any military experience to assist them, and their drill had to be commenced; but they possessed the hereditary courage of their race: they could all ride; many of them were sportsmen, some of them crack shots, and admirable swordsmen. Made of such material, is it to be wondered at that they traversed the most distracted portions of the district in the height of the revolt? – that they fearlessly faced, with the support of two little mountain train guns, manned by native artillerymen of doubtful loyalty, forty native Nujeebs, and forty of the Rifle Regiment, the assembled hordes of one of the most enterprising leaders this rebellion has produced, and, with little or no loss to themselves, routed and destroyed in hundreds the same class of men as those whose unbridled villainy produced such mischief in the station on the night following the outbreak? – that, maddened by the insults and massacres inflicted on their own relations, on their own brothers and sisters, they executed, if let loose on a rebel village, a vengeance which made it a terror and a fear to the country around?

It was deemed at one time desirable that we should have a paper of our own at Meerut, in the shape of a broad sheet printed in the Dum Dumma, giving an epitome of the Kossid's dispatches, service expeditions, and other news of the week. It was to have been styled, in honour of the Corps, "The Literary Dustman;" but as few of those amongst us who could edit the paper had time to devote to it, the project fell to the ground, and, as all Gazettes were then in abeyance, many who are well acquainted with less important services have never heard of the expeditions of the Khakee Ressalah.

Chapter Six

I shall attempt to describe a few of those who held the position of officers or troopers in our volunteer Ressalah; a few only, as the troop reached at one time a muster of fifty. The first of our Khakees in rank was, of course, the Major Commandant. The effect which the atrocities committed by the rebels had on the minds of their former well-wishers was typified in his case. His portly figure, merry black eye, mildness of manner, and uniform kindness to the natives, had given him among the sepoys of his own regiment the name of the "Rajah Sahib." But I have seen him almost frenzied, by the loss of near and dear relatives, look with horror on the entire race, and advocate a retribution which would overwhelm the avengers as well as the former victims, leaving us neither life nor possession, but King Francis's boast alone to be inherited by our memories, – "Tout est perdu sauve l'honneur."

Our second in command was a good specimen of the genuine English gentleman, quiet and retiring in ordinary intercourse, an accomplished draughtsman and a polished writer, but recklessly forward in danger, with a slight and almost feeble frame, but an ardent spirit that knew no fear. He was admirably qualified to conciliate his cavalier following in quarters, and lead the wildest charge in mortal fray.

The Adjutant, third and last of those supposed to hold commissioned rank over the Khakee troopers, was Captain T———, an officer of those Irregular Horsemen who have proved our most inveterate enemies, of powerful frame and unusually handsome features. He fittingly headed, on several occasions, the anomalous troop with which chance had thrown him. His own corps, the 14th Hindostanee Horse, had acquired an infamous notoriety by their atrocities at Jhansi, and his life was only saved by the providential accident of his escorting his wife to the Hills just before the disturbances commenced.

Of the civilians composing the corps, one of the most conspicuous, though but a trooper in the Ressalah, held the rank of Civil and Sessions Judge of one of our most important districts. He much resembled Albert Smith's *Mr. Ledbury*, but aged and experienced, with a high forehead, spectacles, patriarchal beard, and a good-natured gentleness of temper. A known reluctance to punish had characterised him in former official life; but the hardening effects of the mutinies, and the habit which makes a second nature, may be judged of by a scene which occurred in one of our expeditions.

While the Khakees dismounted were forcing their way into a village of rebel Goojurs, one of the latter, who, on the first alarm of an attack, had failed in reaching the village, was found perched high up on a neighbouring tree, and telegraphing to a distant Goojur township for assistance, we being already opposed to four or five times our own numbers. The short carbines of the volunteer troopers failed once or twice in taking effect on the signaller, who, on finding his position and employment observed, commenced a tirade of the foulest vernacular abuse against his assailants. "I will soon stop that noise, my friend," mildly remarked Mr.————, and at the same time quietly raising his rifle, a ball from its unerring groove whistled through the body of the Goojur, who fell with a leaden sound from the tree-top.

A Sikh, au Naturel

S——— again, another of our own subdivision, an ex-Deputy Commissioner of the Punjab, and late Magistrate of Boolundshehur, but at that time, though an exiled potentate, as merry as a cricket, made light of all his misfortunes, and would often relieve the monotony of our weary long night marches by a cantato recitative of "The Ratcatcher's Daughter." This was chiefly amusing from the utter defiance of time and tune with which the subject was treated, and the solemn respect with which it was listened to by the long-bearded Sikhs of our escort.

M———, his assistant, was a cool, high-spirited young fellow, who retained even in India a profound esteem for High Church formula and doctrine, who accepted his official position as a simple matter of course, and took to fighting in the grade of a trooper when the mutinies broke out, as an ordinary step in "natur."

We had a right good representation of the fox-hunters of England, in the joint magistrate of Meerut, commonly called "the Squire," whose Meltonian equipment, and easy seat on horseback, stood him in good stead during our tours. A khakee mess was soon got up, which did much to render our anxious lives more comfortable. Our manner and countenance, when news arrived, were of course closely scanned by our Mussulman table-servants, whose opinions as to the advisability, or otherwise, of quitting our service, would naturally be regulated by the way in which we prospered under our dangers, I have known a despatch, the disasters recorded in which quite prostrated one old officer, picked up and read out aloud by a youngster, amidst shouts of applause from the members of the mess, every fresh loss calling for a renewed cheer, in the fierce determination not to let the native attendants at least chuckle over our depression. A burst of laughter followed the speech of the reader, who, in allusion to the "claret-mug"- circulating round the table, exclaimed, "Well, my lads, when the worst comes to the worst, we will finish with a mug of laudanum."

It is a very different thing laughing at and talking over your troubles in a social circle of Englishmen, to awaiting alone in quiet confidence at some out-station the rising of that tide which must, terminate your existence. Young John Wedderburn, magistrate and collector at the Civil Station of Hissar, though having full intimation of the outbreaks around, could not leave his post with honour, and attending as usual to the routine duties of his profession, was, when the Hurrianah Light Infantry mutinied, shot down in his office.

Our guests at mess were often our comrades in the field, and one of the greatest favourites in either position was Captain Wardlaw, of H.M. 6th Carbineers. He commanded two troops, known as the Crimean squadron of the Dragoon Guards, the men of which were devotedly attached to him. He, poor fellow, fell shortly after on the field of Gungeree, where he had gallantly routed a large body of rebel horse, and captured three guns, by one of the most brilliant cavalry charges which has occurred during this war. On drawing up after riding through the enemy, he took off his helmet, and was calling on his men to give three cheers, when a bullet through the brain caused his instantaneous death. Never died a soldier of more unpretending modesty, or more dashing gallantry:

> *"Mild in manner, far' in favour, fond in friendship, fierce in fight,*
>
> *"Warrior nobler, better, braver, never yet had seen the light."*

It is truly no taint to the manhood of the bronzed veterans who had followed him so long, that they wept bitterly as they laid him in his grave.

The first expedition undertaken by the Volunteers was to certain villages within five miles of cantonments, on the Bhagput road. The fact that these men, within sight almost of our troops, could close the road, plunder the in india in passengers, and collect in hundreds to intimidate or attack neighbouring villages, speaks for itself as to the necessity then existing for a body of "specials with unfettered action."

Two guns and some Carbineers were allowed to accompany the Ressalah. Paunchlee, Ghaut, and Nuggla, three villages principally concerned, were burnt, several Goojurs killed, and of forty prisoners taken thirty-four were hanged by military commission. The day after this affair, revenue collections in the Meerut Pergunnah commenced. Every fresh expedition added to the facility of realising our revenue, and in a few months, amidst the wreck and disorganisation of surrounding districts, the entire government demand had been collected, with a rapidity and completeness hitherto unprecedented.

One of the most active and energetic assistants in this duty was J. C. W———, ex-judge of Moradabad. He had come to Meerut after the mutiny at that station, surrounded by about thirty Sowars of the 8th Irregular Regiment, over whom he exercised an extraordinary influence. They were men of the most dangerous class, Pathan Mussulmans of Rohilcund. Yet W———, refusing to join our Volunteers, rode about the country with these highly suspicious characters, making them escort treasure, or hang criminals, as might be required. That they could be treacherous as the rest of their class was proved by the treason of Nusseer Khan before mentioned; and after the taking of Delhi, numerous letters filled with treasonable conspiracies, and plans for attacking Meerut, were found

in the King's office, written by Kaim Khan, one of W——
—'s principal native officers.

W—— is one of those men whose labours for a
quarter of a century have, as far as his own fame and
fortune is concerned, been nearly thrown away; whereas
his energy and ability, if engaged in any of our colonies,
would have won for him a position and a name.

On the 8th July news of the burning of Begumabad
came into Meerut, and within a few hours the Khakee
Ressalah, accompanied by fifteen of my Nujeebs, twenty
native Christians, armed with muskets and bayonets, and
two small mountain train guns, manned by native
artillerymen, started on an expedition, the origin and
result of which was as follows.

The Goojur village of Seekree, distant about sixteen
miles from Meerut cantonments, on the Delhi road, took
an active part, from the very commencement of our
present disturbances, in the Dacoitees and disgraceful
butcheries for which their tribe has become notorious.
The first act by which they marked their defiance of all
legitimate authority, was the seizure of a five Biswa
portion of the neighbouring village of Kazimpoor,
belonging to some Hindoo Faqueers (Byragees), killing
seven of them. Soon after, supposing that their practices
found impunity, they drove out the police of the
Begumabad Chowkee.

A number of Jâts commenced collecting at the
important village of Begumabad, for the propose of
defending themselves against the three Goojur villages of
Seekree, Nuggla, and Deosa; but this was met by a counter
collection of Goojurs, not only of those three villages, but
others in the neighbourhood. The Goojurs very rapidly
outnumbered the Jâts, being better armed, less divided

amongst themselves, and more habituated to acts of violence. The Goojurs very soon disclosed their intention of attacking the Jâts at Begumabad, destroying the village, and plundering the bazar. Urgent solicitations for assistance were sent to Meerut by the parties threatened; but there being much important work, of apparently more immediate necessity, to employ the Ressalah, we were obliged to tell them that they must defend themselves for a time, but that they might count on our taking steps when possible to assist them. The news of this fact probably went to Seekree, as well as to. Begumabad, and at nine o'clock at night, on the 8th inst., information was received that the attack on Begumabad had taken place that day, and the usual ruthless atrocities been committed; the Jâts, greatly outnumbered, scarcely offering any resistance.

The district Volunteers had been ordered to parade at two o'clock for service that night, in another direction; but the course of events having rendered prompt punishment of the rebels of Seekree all important, the march was altered for that village.

The suddenness of our advent defied even the vigilance of the Goojur intelligence department. By grey dawn we had reached the ruins of Begumabad.

A drenching rain had set in, which lasted all day. The fires were still smouldering in the bazar on the roadside, the Government chowkee and the dawk bungalow tenantless, with only blackened walls standing, the flooring in many places dug up, while here and there in the fields wandered a few miserable fugitives from the village. At this point Captain D'O——, taking eleven of the Europeans and three Sikhs with him, set out at a gallop for the village of Seekree, distant about two miles. We swept rapidly round the village, leaving two or three horsemen at various points to encircle it; no inhabitant was in sight, and our encirclement was completed ere the first few startled villagers appeared.

Armed men rapidly collected; the small number of the advanced guard had the appearance of a magistrate's party attempting an ordinary arrest, and within a few seconds of our arrival a crowd of men, women, and children issued, the men shouting defiance and brandishing their swords. A few carbine shots taking effect in the crowd, drove them back to cover, whence they commenced an ineffectual fire with matchlocks, the fuses of which were soon put out by the rain.

Our party numbering five only, about twenty men pushed past us. Captain T——— had, however, galloped off in advance of the guns with a few district volunteers, and noting the movements of the Goojurs, cut off and killed thirteen men of the few who obtained an exit.

Major W——— meanwhile having brought up a small twelve-pounder howitzer, opened with shot, shell, and carcases; the rain, however, prevented the thatches igniting, and a strong body of Goojurs were seen collecting in a large double-storied mud huveilee.

Our only foot-men, excepting those by the guns, were some musicians of the late 11th N.I. and fifteen Nujeebs. These not being sufficiently well disciplined for the work, Captain T——— dismounted some of the Ressalah, and led them into the village, to carry the huveilee, the howitzer being brought in to blow open the doorway. Here considerable resistance was at first offered, and Captain D'O———, who had exposed himself much throughout, being struck by a splintered ball in the throat, fell on his sword, cutting his left hand severely. The door being found impracticable, Captain T———'s party scaled the walls, and rapidly destroyed all men within the place, two more of our party only getting wounded. The village was then effectually fired, and the assembly sounded, five hours having elapsed from the commencement of the attack, and all women and children having been carefully protected throughout.

The Jâts who followed had been so cowed by their losses of the previous day that they were useless, except for plunder, hundreds of them flying from a few Goojurs.

Two of the party distinguished themselves, but in a very different way: the one, a little dentist, whose military predilection and pluck ought to have placed him in the army; and the other a gentleman who would be styled an Italian or Spaniard as a euphonium for a bronzed complexion in Europe, but whom we class in this country, by ambiguous metaphor, as an "Arabian."

The dentist fairly earned the mural crown: for when the scaling party got to the roof of a house abutting against the walled enclosure where the principal Goojurs were, he requested me to give him a lift, and being but a light weight, I quickly sent him over the wall, where he stood a good chance of receiving the contents of any spare matchlocks that might be ready. Some volunteers in the crowd having performed a similar friendly turn to myself, and our party being augmented by a few more lifts from outside to some seven or eight, our revolvers and swords soon settled matters with its defenders.

I have often noticed that the courage of the native, (unlike that of the European, which rises with his difficulties,) is invariably in proportion to his hopes of success; that individuals, if accompanied by an overwhelming force, will frequently do acts of bravery, though they will abjectly submit to destruction without resistance, if their assailants attack with determination and in any but insignificant numbers. Their cruelty to the vanquished is not proportioned to the difficulties they have gone through, the dangers they have encountered, or the resistance they have met, but is often greatest when their victims are most helpless, or their own feeling of security from punishment most complete.

Similar tactics in an inferior sphere may be seen practiced in any of the temple-groves inhabited by monkeys in India. The initiatory manoeuvre to a single combat by one of these caricatures of the human or Hindustani species, is a horrible face and a hurried advance of one or two steps towards his opponent. Should tins masterly opening of the campaign have the desired effect, and his enemy manifest decided infirmity of purpose, or a desire to retreat, number one pursues his advantage with a commendable energy and vigour, rushing on with a courage bordering on reckless indifference to danger; but should the original stare of defiance be returned by a contortion of simian visage even a shade more diabolical than that of the attacking party, and possibly a threatened approach, the moral influence of this "firm front" is immediately recognised in the sudden collapse and ignominious rout of number one. The saying, that "a coward will fight at bay," seldom applies in this country. "A Bahadoor brought to bay, grows a coward," would be more correct.

The Arabian equestrian above alluded to, who had been for some time keeping up his courage and keeping out the rain by repeated libations of ration rum, was seized with a sudden desire for martial distinction; but unable to discriminate very clearly between friend and foe, shot one of our unfortunate Jât auxiliaries through the head. He was of course promptly deprived of his weapons, and was finally sent off to Meerut by Palkee Gharree, in a state of "coma," possibly of "clairvoyance."

Chapter Seven

The station of Meerut was defended principally by the "Duma Dumma," or fortified enclosure (formerly the field-magazine and Artillery school of instruction) at one end, and two fortified hospital enclosures belonging to the 60th Royal Rifles at the other. On three sides of the Dura Dumma, the parapet and ditch abutted against the old brick-wall of the Compound; but on the fourth, or entrance side, the parapet was at a sufficient distance to allow of a metalled road between it and the wall, as an approach to the gate. In the batteries and at the gateway were invariably stationed sentinels of the 60th Royal Rifles, who enforced with most rigid strictness the military rules as to parole and password. The admirable discipline of these men was a constant theme of admiration in both Delhi and Meerut. However severe or harassing their duties, however decimating or destructive the skirmishes or operations in which they were engaged, the remnant on duty invariably presented the same clean, active, obedient, and soldierly carriage. I have seen regiments grow slovenly under discomfort and difficulty, and feel confident that every relaxation of discipline is prejudicial alike to the health, comfort, and contentment of the soldier. The 60th Royal Rifles appeared throughout every stage of the disturbance, and their own glorious services, quiet and respectful, but smart, active, and efficient.

The inside of the Dum Dumma presented a strange mixture of martial and domestic arrangements; many touches of nature, quaint or melancholy. Little English children played merrily around the piles of shrapnel, round shot, and shell. English ladies worked quietly in the brick-paved barrack-rooms and laboratories, or dined mess-fashion at the rough benches and settles made for the soldiery. They were the sisters of those whose heroism at Lucknow placed the names of gentle Englishwomen on the records of military fame; and many there would have met the privations and sufferings of close investment with the same thorough-bred courage with which they smiled at the troubles and privations of what was little better than a state of siege. The inner guards and patrolling of the Dum Dumma were performed by a volunteer company of footmen, chiefly old pensioners and Eurasians; the latter, a mixed race partly European and partly of coloured or Hindustani origin, showed their anomalous ancestry in their mental conformation as clearly as their complexion; some of them exhibiting a ludicrous objection to running any personal risks, others by their gallantry giving unmistakable proof of their paternal descent.

One redoubtable warrior of the former class, a Mr. Barkis, whose portly figure and dignified deportment had long secured him a position as distinguished as that of Mr. Turvydrop, in the far-off regions of his ancestors, was led by the combined influence of patriotism and other exciting stimulants, rashly to enrol himself in the devoted band of intramural volunteers. His enthusiasm in his novel position, and the wholesome excitements above alluded to, even caused him, with a vaguely indefinite allocution, but a stern and decisive manner, to demand the "post of danger." This post not being brought to him, may, perhaps, have been the cause of the remarkable variation in his opinion, which took place the same evening, as to the accuracy of the old Horatian adage, *Dulce et decorum est pro patria mori.* The exciting scenes of the period had probably brought the nervous system of Mr. Barkis into an abnormal and irritable condition.

At the evening parade a musket-shot, and the sharp ping of a bullet (a very ordinary sound at that time, owing to the frequent advent of marauding Goojurs into cantonments) was followed by a sudden vacancy in the ranks, and the subsidence in comatose helplessness of Mr. Barkis, his immediate removal to the hospital-ward, and a careful superficial examination by the surgeon ensued. This was a tedious operation, owing to the extent of surface to be examined; but as no wound could be discovered, the subdued and sensitive Mr. Barkis was declared "fit for service," and ordered out that very night on picket duty. As the guard filed out through the gate, Mr. Barkis declared that he had volunteered for service inside the Dum Dumma, and looked on their present expedition as rash and objectionable. Some ominous allusion on the part of the officer in command to corporal punishment and military execution, led the unwilling Mr. Barkis to that post which in an unguarded moment he had rashly called for: the result was melancholy in the extreme.

Anxiety has been known to attenuate with marvellous rapidity the most robust frame; but seldom has the malady known by physicians as *timor irrationalis* produced a more complete absorption, or rather abstraction of the whole corporeal system, than in the present instance. When the relief went out, a musket and bayonet were found at the sentry-post, but no trace of Mr. Barkis could be discovered, and the authorities, perhaps wisely, did not institute any commission to investigate the phenomenon of his disappearance: like Sam Weller's celebrated sausage-maker, "he never was a heerd on arterwards."

Sadly solemn, however, was the appearance of the room

in which Divine service used to be held on a Sunday: many of its occupants were clothed in mourning for late and sudden bereavements; many a widowed mother awaited in hopeful anxiety the possibility of a return to the country of her friends and family; many of the men bore scars scarce closed of wounds received on the night of the outbreak; and the often repeated ritual of the English Liturgy and Sacramental service, had a speaking vitality for those whose position was even then one of great danger, and whose destruction must inevitably have followed any reverse to our arms on retirement from before Delhi.

I believe that so long as the siege lasted, while the question of our ability to hold our own before the imperial city was doubtful, there was not a spot in the North-West more safe than – certainly none in the Doab so safe as – the Delhi camp. The men there had their almost daily skirmishing with the enemy, and their chance of wounds and death in fair service, or of a perilous retreat; but their retreat must have been certain massacre for the handful of Europeans occupying stations in the Doab. Few can realise, except those who have experienced it, the unnatural excitability and anxiety produced on the mind under such circumstances, when day after day brought news of "no progress before Delhi." The seeming utter stagnation at one time, and at others the interruption of all communication with the camp, and the hourly expectation of important revolts, while the delay before Delhi swallowed up months, produced a feeling which made active service of any kind, for every ardent mind at least, a blessing, and led all officers who had any chance of success to apply for employment in the camp.

Chapter Eight

Few persons in England are aware what the ordinary duties and responsibilities of District Officers are, and still fewer the positions they frequently held, and the duties they had to perform, during the disturbances. They had to collect information and to report constantly to military authority; they had to declare cases of misconduct and rebellion, and apply for military aid, when available, to crush the germs of revolt, or to raise and lead irregulars of their own against the rebels.

On all expeditions, undertaken either with or without their concurrence, they had to accompany the troops, to provide supplies, and, in many instances, had the unenviable task of singly and alone protesting against indiscriminate or injudicious punishment of villages. They were the tribunes of the people, and, actuated by similar indignation against the brethren of the mutineers, had to bear the opprobrium of supporting those whom they deemed innocent, or "not committed," against their countrymen roused to madness, and utterly ignorant of the numberless shades of distinction, or the antecedents of native communities or individuals, familiar to themselves. As an instance, however, of the serious mischief likely to arise from entrusting, even under martial law, absolute authority to men destitute of all local experience, and utterly ignorant of civil administration, I will record an instance which occurred just after my return to Meerut.

Between Meerut and Bhagput, on the road to the Delhi camp, there is a Rajpoot village called Deolah, by the

Eastern Jumna Canal. On the occasion of my riding in from Delhi, Nawul Sing, one of the chief men of the village, with a number of his relations, came out to meet me. I knew the place well, having on former occasions pitched my camp there.

The Rajpoots pointed out to me with pride that they had protected and preserved the Canal Station near their village. The Deputy-Superintendent of the Canal, a native, was living with them. One half-caste, and one European woman, had, in their flight from Delhi, received shelter in the village: one of these was in it at the time, preferring to stay there rather than go into Meerut. The large Government mango-garden, in which the fruit was nearly ripe, had been carefully preserved from spoliation; they also restored a Government cavalry horse which a mutineer trooper had ridden to a standstill near the village.

Some time after my return to Meerut, I found it necessary to send the Government post by camel dawk past Deolah to camp. On one occasion the Mussulman camel-rider walked into the garden, and commenced helping himself to the mangoes. He was quickly turned out by the Deolah men, but swore he would be revenged. He then returned to Meerut, and reported to the military authorities that he had been stopped between Deolah and Joonmanee on his road to camp. This was, of course, a most serious charge. The nearest villages were usually made responsible for such crimes; but no reference was made to me on the subject, though my acquaintance with the people would have enabled me easily to sift and expose the camel-man's story.

Complete independence and indiscriminate vigour appear to be the soul of martial law. A detachment of troops was to pass the villages along the road to camp, and the commanding officer was ordered to burn the villages of Joonmanee and Deolah, to seize the head man and execute him, the order expressly stating that "no mercy was to be shown to this man." Poor Nawul Sing little thought what a fitting reward we had found for his loyal conduct since the mutinies. Fortunately, however, an intelligent young Civil officer, Mr. S———, happened to accompany the detachment on his way to camp, and he was partially entrusted with the execution of the sentence, subordinate of course to the officer commanding the detachment; but being a complete stranger to the district, he could not, except accidentally, or as fortuitous circumstances ordained, be of much service.

The village of Joonmanee was duly burnt, and this I was not sorry for, as the people, though quite innocent of the crime for which the punishment was inflicted, were noted for their bad character even before the disturbances. On the party proceeding to Deolah, however, the half-caste woman whom they had sheltered came out to plead for them, and declared that the inhabitants, very far from attempting to stop Government dawks, had uniformly been well affected. Mr. S——— had been for some time living in the Dum Dumma, and remembered that he had heard the name of the village of Deolah favourably mentioned for their kindness to Delhi fugitives, and, exercising a wise discretion, he prevented the execution of the sentence. I was naturally indignant on hearing that little but an accident had saved us the humiliation and disgrace of the destruction of a loyal village, and the execution of one of our friends. I afterwards appointed Nawul Sing a Tehsil Jemadar, and there is every prospect of his Rajpoots being nobly rewarded by Government. The camel-man unfortunately made himself scarce on hearing that I had got hold of his case.

A startling prescience and judgment is shown in some

of Lord Ellenborough's speeches made on the breaking out of the disturbances; and I observed soon after a declaration of his to the effect, that civil administration might possibly in some districts be rendered almost impracticable by the effects of the eccentric operations of martial law.

Finding it absolutely essential that our enterprising enemy Sah Mull should be crushed, and a lesson inflicted on the rebel Goojurs and Mussulmans of Pergunnah Burout, whose proximity to Delhi rendered their management difficult, I had outlined a plan for attacking the southern villages by a rapid advance from Meerut of the Khakee Ressalah, and such help as the General would give us. It was certain that considerable danger attended the attempt, as forces would certainly be sent after us from Delhi; but I trusted to the rapidity of our movements, the increasing distance from Delhi as we advanced on Sah Mull's stronghold, and the prestige inseparable from audacity for success. Our worthy commandant of Volunteers objected to the plan as rash, and proposed inverting it, making the Begum Sombre's place of Sirdhana our first stage. The Commissioner's support carried my plan, and, aided by a favouring fortune, we gained the greatest success ever won by our Volunteers.

In the latter end of July, two mountain-guns (manned by two sergeants and eight Golundazes), fifty mounted Volunteers, forty H. M. 60th Rifles, two sergeants and twenty armed musicians, and twenty-seven Nujeebs, marched from Meerut and encamped at Dulhowra, opposite Buleynee, on the banks of the Hindun river, about fifteen miles above the scene of Colonel Sir Archdale Wilson's battles of the Hindun. As our handful of men lay at Dulhowra, heavy firing commenced in the direction of Deolah, only seven miles distant. The distinct and rapid roll of heavy jezails and matchlocks, intermixed with the sullen booming of the guns of Delhi, little more than twenty miles south-east of us, formed a fitting lullaby for those who were next morning to ford the Hindoo and enter a territory from which we fully expected some of us never would return. Nawul Sing, of Deolah, who accompanied us, was sent across to ascertain the cause of the firing. He brought back, during the night, information that Sah Mull and his men lay at the Mussulman village of Bussowd, and intended next day to punish Deolah. We had just arrived in time to save it, as the Rajpoots, native like, were expending their ammunition in trying to frighten away Sail Mull with noise only. During the night an express from Meerut brought us the news of Havelock's advance from Allahabad, and the astonished residents of Dulhowra were awoke by the ringing cheers that followed the announcement.

The reveille aroused us after a brief rest to ford the river, and as grey dawn broke we were nearing Deolah, whence the cavalry went on at a gallop to surround Bussowd. Sah Mull had lost heart, thinking that the number with him, though as ten to one of our party, were not able to cope with the dreaded Feringhees.

A number of the rebels followed their chief; and as the advanced guard of our column swept round the place, matchlockmen and swordsmen, old and young, were streaming out of the doomed village. The women and children seem to have been sent away prior to our arrival, a sure sign that their lords were prepared for the worst. Traces of Sah Mull's commissariat were found, and large stores of grain were collected for the Delhi rebels in Bussowd.

A severe example was essential, and the slightest mawkish pusillanimity in such a case would have spread the flame of revolt throughout the district. All men, therefore, able to carry arms were shot down or put to the sword, and their residences burnt. The only prisoners taken, some fifteen in number, were ordered out of camp and executed in the evening, by order of the Military Commandant of the expedition; and Sah Mull now learnt that the sword alone could atone for his crimes; that he had roused a vengeance which could, when required, equal the sternest retribution he could inflict, women and children alone being exempted from destruction.

His messengers that night traversed every village of the Chowrassee Des, calling all who could bear arms to assist him, and declaring that Sah Mull would meet the pale-faced invaders of his territory on the morrow, and annihilate the entire party, or die in the attempt. Urgent requisitions for help were sent to the King of Delhi, and the next day a couple of mutineer regiments, 150 Sowars and four 9-pounder guns left Delhi for Deolah, but videttes and spies kept us well informed of the enemy's movements. Of our two native Sowars on picket at Ratoul on the Delhi road, one only returned, declaring that his companion had been carried off by the enemy's cavalry patrol. He, however, being a Mussulman, had probably deserted to the enemy.

We marched at twelve at night for Burout; and when the advanced guard of the Delhi troops reached Deolah, finding no trace of our visit but the smoking ruins of Bussowd, they retraced their steps towards Ghazeeoodeen Nugger.

No revenue had been collected from the Burout Pergunnah since the commencement of the outbreak; and as our civil establishments had been driven out of Burout, the collection of supplies at that place became difficult. I therefore determined, as the line of troops moved away along the banks of the Eastern Jumna Canal, to adopt another course parallel with that of the force, and, taking the Tehsildar Kurum Ali and two Sowars with me, visit all the villages near the left bank of the canal. I had proposed arresting all Lumbardars or chief men of the different villages who had not paid their revenue, and collecting sheep and supplies for camp as I went along, trust to my prestige as District Officer for immunity from attack.

Two of my Hindoostanee Nujeebs seeing me leave the troop, followed on small ponies, which they had obtained amongst the spoils of Bussowd, carrying their muskets and bayonets over their shoulders. The first two or three villages I entered were totally deserted; no signs in them of life save a few pariah dogs, who raised a dismal howling at the unwonted loneliness of their position. Heads were sometimes raised here and there amongst the dense cultivation, and the owners rapidly concealed themselves if called to.

Various symptoms showed how rapidly the neglect of this part of the district had led to the belief that the British rule had terminated for ever. One of the first villages I entered was Chowpara, inhabited by Tugga Brahmins. They had all fled, and I was unable to get any representative of the community. The next village of Jaffrabad had also been abandoned; we, however, got hold of a man belonging to it, and sent him off to reassure the Zemindars. I then came to the Goojur village of Bichpooree: this had taken an active part in all Sah Mull's misdoings, and deserved destruction; but as the force had a long march before it, we had not made arrangements to attack it. I, however, went to the village, thinking I might arrest the Lumbardar and secure the "Jumma." Numbers of armed men were leaving it as I arrived; and I told one of the Nujeebs who had voluntarily followed me, to catch

81

one of the fugitives if he could, and make him show me the Lumbardar's house. The footman, however, whom he went up to, cut him down, wounding him in two places, but paying the penalty with his life directly after at our hands.

Having no Europeans with me, I was obliged to give up the intention of arresting the Lumbardar. The shots fired during this episode were heard by the detachment on the canal bank, and a small party came out to reconnoitre and assist me if necessary, returning when they found the matter already settled by an unusually short and sharp magisterial proceeding.

The Commandant, Major W———, sent an old Ressaldar aide-de-camp who was with him, to increase my escort and probably assist me with advice on points of military strategy.

It is a sort of axiom or received dogma among military men that no amount of study and campaigning, no course of amateur evolution or drill, can gift a civilian with the inspiration for command, which Ensign Fitz Eustace acquires by pocketing his commission and putting on his red coat; assuming, in fact, a professional judgment, which society willingly accords to doctors, lawyers, and engineers, by virtue of their especial education, and which will soon, let us hope, be to some extent justified by the system of training and examination now commenced in the army.

It is fortunate, perhaps, that the English public is independent in judgment on such subjects; that they do not recognise the exclusive capacity of − though they bestow to a great extent exclusive light to military command on − those only who enter the military profession by the Horse Guards, or the India House

Military Department; and the services of such men as Clive, and John Lawrence, as military chiefs, and the examples of Ricketts, Wake, Hume, and Palmer, as gallant captains of outposts, have thus been rendered possible. To return to our former subject, however.

I passed through Ghuteea, Sâdoolapoor, Allawulpoor, and Andreespoor, taking one or more Lumbardars with me from each village as security for the Government revenue. These villages appeared glad to see the Tehsildar; and were, I believe, well affected towards us. I took the opportunity of purchasing twelve sheep for "Russud," so had a considerable train to take care of when we arrived at the friendly village of Burka, Here, however, we found all the inhabitants swarming out of their houses, and the gates closed. On recognising the Tehsildar, they came out and whispered a warning to him, that he should fly as fast as possible after the troops, as the whole of the "Chowrassee Des" was being raised by Sah Mull for an attack on us.

While laughing and chatting with these men, and ridiculing to them the "Black Douglas" Sah Mull, a tremendous noise of shouting, bellowing, and other incomprehensible sounds commenced in the neighbouring village of Huldwanie.

The Burka men quickly disappeared inside their intrenched village, and closed the gates. The unfortunate Lumbardars with me looked panic-struck; and as Sah Mull in person, with two thousand of his relations and followers, streamed out of Huldwanie, and rapidly neared our little party, the Tehsildar feelingly begged of me to exhibit that 'discretion which is the better part of valour.' Flight from villagers, in. whatever numbers, was rather a shock to dignity; but, as there was no help for it, I called on the Tehsildar and Ressaldar to remember their positions, and retire quietly.

A volley of matchlock balls interrupted my speech, and a confused mob of armed men approached us. The Ressaldar called out to me that I could do no good by stopping, and tried the experiment of the force of example in a rapid retreat, as his verbal eloquence was not persuasive. Taking a last fond look at the twelve sheep and fifteen Lumbardars whom I had with such difficulty collected, I followed my retreating companions, accompanied by sundry flowers of rhetoric, in which the Hindoostanee language is rich, and which were gracefully accorded to me by Sah Mull's men.

I had got out of gunshot of this rabble, when I perceived a horseman fast coming up to us, his matchlock in one hand and a drawn sword in the other. I had only that morning recovered for Government three troop horses of the 3rd Light Cavalry. I was trying one of them, a young iron-grey, and the trial had nigh cost me my life. The brute possessed an insane terror of fire-arms, either from never having heard them in such proximity before, or from having had unpleasant experience of the effects of gunshot wounds. When I perceived that my over-impetuous friend, the Sowar, had placed a sufficient distance between himself and his party to give me hopes of disposing of him without interference, and I had checked and wheeled my horse round for the purpose, the animal proceeded to the charge alternately tripping along sideways, or waltzing round on its hind legs, springing clear off the ground at every discharge of my revolver. I had implicit confidence, from long practice, in my own pistol shooting and fencing; but I can defy any one not trained to acrobatic performances to have done anything more than hold on with that ever-to-be-anathematised grey.

My progress must, I have often thought since, have had a ludicrous appearance, resembling the performances of Astley's professionals in their combats with some renowned Pagan. I was able, however, by good luck, to remove the thumb of my opponent's sword-hand, and mortally wound his horse. In drawing my slight double-edged sword, however, (my horse having at the moment adopted an angle of ninety degrees, as the most suitable slope for his back,) I managed to draw blood from my own throat.

The footmen and others under Sah Mull, in the meanwhile, having come up and materially added to the effect of the circus-like fight by a desultory discharge of matchlocks, I made the best of my way after my companions, abandoning to my opponent and his friends my pith helmet, which had come off in the melee, as a slight remuneration for the thumb and charger of which I had deprived him. I afterwards ascertained that the horseman with whom I had this skirmish was one Bugda, nephew to Sah Mull, and a general in the service of the titular King of Delhi.

Our next grand object was to find out where the detachment might be; and supposing that it must by that time have reached Burout, the Tehsildar made straight for that place. On reaching it, I found the two mountain guns left with only four men of the 60th Rifles, under Dr. C——, who informed me that the column had been already attacked by a party of rebels from Mullutpore, who, it appears, were on their way to the general rendezvous under Sah Mull. Some of them had entered the city of Burout, opposite which the riflemen were drawn up, shots flashed now and then from the flat housetops, and the Khakees were nowhere to be seen, they having dashed off in pursuit of some of the Mullutpore men who had not entered the town. I learnt that as the column was entering the place on their way to the Tehsil, where we proposed encamping, they were met by a discharge of small-arms. One old white-bearded Sikh, who had long lived in Mullutpore, and therefore led the rebels, made himself conspicuous by his repeated attempts to accomplish a successful shot with his matchlock. This man I recognised and hanged, some months afterwards, when on a visit to Burout.

I had reported matters to the Major, and the Khakee Ressalah were just arriving, when shouting and firing near our guns told us that my Huldwanie acquaintances had arrived. They had occupied a grove of trees, and a garden inclosure close to us. The Rifles were, therefore, pushed on, and the Volunteers brought up at a gallop and placed on their flanks. The enemy kept up a smart fire at first, which the handful of riflemen, in skirmishing order, returned; but as soon as the latter commenced closing with them, and they found both flanks being turned by the two little parties of horsemen, they broke and fled in all directions.

As we swept through the fields, now dotted all over with fugitives, the Khakees themselves being completely scattered in the excitement of pursuit, the usual cutting and pointing commenced in all directions. My horse having recovered from the effects of the revolver going off just over his head, I took care to keep to the sword only; which, as the enemy's matchlocks were all discharged, was quite sufficient.

A regular Hindoostanee Sowar has no chance against a good English fencer. They can parry a cut well, but never attempt to parry the thrust. I saw two of our party lose their horses from desperate sword-cut wounds, inflicted by a swordsman, who sprang up in a sugar-cane field; but this was from bad management on their part. Instead of putting spurs to their horses and riding straight at him with the thrust, they turned short round, avoiding the cuts themselves, but got their horses so injured they had to be destroyed. A Duffadar of my Nujeeb footmen, a very gallant fellow, sprang at the man and pinioned his arms in his own; he, however, seized one of the Nujeeb's arms with his teeth, and compelled him to relinquish his hold, then struck him down with a blow on the head, receiving a similar sword-cut at the same moment himself. Both men were down on the ground when one of the Rifles went up, and as the Duffadar unfortunately was not in uniform, he fired his rifle into him, and drove his bayonet through his opponent.

I happened to be on the left bank, but those on the right had the good fortune to come up with Sail Mull himself and several of his relatives. The former was killed by a young Volunteer, by name Tonnochy, assisted by an Irregular horseman; and from one of the men, who was shot off a camel, my helmet was recovered; not before it was wanted, as the sun was dangerously powerful. Sah Mull's head being stuck on a pole, inspired our native friends in Burout with mingled satisfaction and dread.

I now set to work to provide supplies for the troops, and was sitting on the site chosen for our camp, with the Tehsildar, when the rapid and repeated discharge of our little mountain train guns, mixed with musketry-firing, made us jump on our horses and hurry a second time to the spot, where we found the rebels had returned to the attack, but were easily driven off with grape. It is probable that few of those who made this, the third attack of the day, knew of Sah Mull's death; and the sight of his head on a pole behind our guns probably aided materially in routing them, and preventing any further attack.

The Bunyahs of Burout gladly brought us supplies on seeing Sah Mull defeated, and we encamped that evening in and around a bungalow belonging to a deputy-superintendent of the Eastern Jumna Canal, which Sah Mull had preserved as a hall of justice for himself. There were 165 natives killed at Seekree, upwards of 150 at Bussowd, and probably about the same number in the above skirmishes at Burout.

Chapter Nine

It was evident that though we might defy the assaults of the villages round Burout, we should all be cut off if they were joined by regulars and guns from Delhi. Sah Mull's nephew had gone to the Mâvee Jât village of Sirsullee, where he was again collecting the rebels of the Chowrassee Dês, for an attack on us.

At midnight, therefore, the word was passed round for rousing quietly the men asleep about the bungalow; and within an hour the whole party trooped silently away, crossing the ditch of the town on their way to Hurra, *en route* for Sirdhana.

As I believed the Tehsildar Kurm. Ali knew the road, I proposed to the Major that I should go on with him and a couple of orderlies, as a feeling party. I found, after going some distance, that the rebels of that quarter had, probably in order to show their hatred of made roads as a Feringhee institution, ploughed up and sown a considerable portion of the one we were to traverse. I halted at the edge of the cultivation, and waited till the column came up, running the risk of being shot for my pains, as I did not hear them challenge, and they mistook us in the dark for rebel Sowars. I then moved on considerably in advance, passing in dead silence the rebel village of Johwree. This march was the most fatiguing I ever experienced; and even after day broke, no sign of our approach to the Burnawa Ghat, at which we were to ford the Krishnee and Hindun rivers, appeared. Our party of five halted for some time, in hopes that the column would arrive; but they also were not to be seen, and the country, though well cultivated, seemed almost uninhabited. We could not, of course, with our small number, attempt to visit any of the villages, as we could not tell whether they might, or might not, be then gathering under Sujja Ram.

We began to have an unpleasant conviction that we had lost our road; and soon after, meeting a native carrying a bundle of wood, we asked him where the road we were on would lead us? "To Sirsullee," he replied, adding, that it was only four miles off, and that Burnawa Ghât was in the opposite direction. We could not believe him at first, though his statement was perfectly true; and had we gone on to Sirsullee, Sujja Ram and his followers would have made short work of our little party.

A sharp gallop brought us soon back to the track of the column, which we caught up just as they were fording the rivers. We carried a small silken union-jack as the banner of the Volunteers, and on this occasion an ensign also, in the shape of Sah Mull's gory head stuck on a long spear. This last was necessary, to prove to the country-people, who knew the sternly resolute features of the old ruffian well, that their leader was really dead.

At Hurra, we heard of the arrival in a neighbouring village of reinforcements from Meerut, two Horse Artillery guns, and a party of Carbineers, who had orders to hold the Ghat for us. They had been marching, like ourselves, all night; but not having any of the Meerut district officers with them, and the Ranghur village of Kiwai, at which they halted, being badly affected, they had nothing to eat.

When I rode over in the evening, the soldiers had been starving for nearly twenty-four hours; but English soldiers are wonderfully helpless as to foraging, bivouacking, and cooking, unless the commissariat is complete. I at once entered the village to arrest the head men, telling them that they would be paid if they brought food, and their houses fired if they did not. Seeing a couple of calves careering about, I seized one, and one of my orderlies another: these we presented to the Carbineers, who helplessly remarked, "that they could not do anything with them, as they had no knives to cut them up with." Imagine a Zouave, with a long sword at his side, making such a speech!

On our arrival at Sirdhana, we occupied the palace, and the men were regaled with a breakfast of curry and rice, prepared by the Tehsildar of the place. Sirdhana was formerly the residence of the old Begum Sombre, who adopted the children of an adventurer named Colonel Dyce, whose son, under the name of Mr. Dyce Sombre, is well known in England. The palace, a handsome building, but badly situated, is now the property of his widow. There is also a very large cathedral in the Italian style, built by the old Begum after her conversion to Roman Catholicism. These two handsome piles, which rise most incongruously amidst mud huts, and by an Indian bazar, have wonderfully escaped all injury during the outbreak. Pickets and patrols were of course placed round the palace at night, during our stay.

Sundry reports of a meditated attack by Rajpoots and others, to recover Sah Mull's head, reached us during the day, and gave rise to a scene of dire confusion. The same night a sudden alarm among the Rifles was heard, which rapidly increased in noise and confusion to a tumult. One of the riflemen, running into the palace from his post, exclaimed, "that the rebels were bayoneting our men in numbers at the gate." A voice on the flight of steps leading to the entrance-hall, shouted to the cavalry-men within, "Carbineers, take to your swords," and out they went pell-mell. Some of the riflemen, who could not in the dark get hold of their bayonets, commenced pummelling each other with their fists, and the officer in command found himself going gravely through the parry and thrust with one of his own men, armed with a fixed bayonet. The man, on recognising him, touched his hat, saying apologetically, "Why, sir, I really thought you was an Ingen." The disorder, however, subsided almost as rapidly as it had arisen, and was found to have been caused by a little bugler, who, getting nightmare from his long march and heavy breakfast of the morning, had commenced yelling in his sleep.

I had embraced the opportunity of our force lying in Sirdhana to despatch Chuprassies, with orders for the payment of arrears of revenue, to all the neighbouring villages. The chief of the Rajpoots in the neighbourhood, Rhydul of Rardhuna, came into camp and made arrangements for the payment of his arrears. The men of Ukulpoora, however, which belonged to his relative Nirput Sing, sent back my messengers with an inquiry, who the district officer and Tehsildar were, that they should demand revenue from Ukulpoora; threatening the messengers with death if ever they came back on such an errand to them. Now, Nirput Sing had before been noted for his attack on the Sirdhana Tehsil, previously mentioned. He and his followers had filled up the measure of their offences. Our force, therefore, started before daybreak to pay him a visit. The alarm rapidly spread through the neighbourhood that the "Khakees were out;" and by the time we reached Rardhuna, its inhabitants, thinking themselves doomed to destruction, commenced beating their dhôl, or Indian war-drum, and turning out in numbers. I immediately rode forward and addressed them in Hindoostanee to the effect that they should not make fools of themselves; that Rhydul had declared himself for Government, and that we would not hurt them, having "other fish to fry." They dispersed immediately, delighted to hear that they were not the objects of our vengeance.

Ukulpoora was only a short distance off, and I began to be afraid that Nirput Sing might escape us. Our commanding officer unfortunately heard the drum, however, which had seriously excited his choler; and, to my great disgust, the force was halted, the guns unlimbered, and every preparation for an attack on Rardhuna commenced. As I had ordered off the villagers, I rode up and remonstrated against the folly of allowing the avowed rebel, Nirput Sing, to escape by wasting time in destroying the village of a chief who on more than one occasion had shown himself friendly to us; to say nothing of the bad effects on the natives, of such utter want of discrimination as inflicting vengeance for the insult of drum-beating, in preference to embracing the opportunity of destroying an outlaw.

The men were with difficulty moved on, and we were fortunate in surrounding Ukulpoora, with Nirput Sing and the other Thakoors in it. They armed and collected about his house, but after a few discharges of shrapnel and grape from the guns, the Rifles entered the village, shooting and bayoneting all they met; the women and children having been removed, evidently in the expectation that an attack would be made. Nirput Sing, a strikingly handsome specimen of the Rajpoot, lay in the midst of the slain; though his father, an old man, had come out after the village was surrounded, to assure us solemnly that he was not in it.

The force was then marched in triumph through the

village of Rardhuna, the offending drum being brought out and destroyed in the Major's presence. The punishment of Ukulpoora had an excellent effect on the turbulent spirits around, and they remained quiet afterwards, even when the neighbouring pergunnah of Mozuffernugger was in flames.

On the return of the Khakees to Meerut, we were joined by several cavalry officers, who, though very shy of having anything to do with us at first, did us the honour of enlisting in our ranks as troopers, after hearing of our hard work in the Chowrasse Dês.

I returned once again to Sirdhana, but had to go there without the Khakees, as they were employed at Haupper, watching the rebel chief of Malagurh. The Mozuffernugger district was in a very disturbed state; and news having reached us that a large number of Mussulmans, and Mavee Jâts, and others, were collecting from Binowlee and Prassowlee at a place called Boorhana, with the intention of plundering the Palace and Cathedral, I started with my joint magistrate, W———, and an Irish gentleman named Murphy, but with police horsemen and Nujeebs only as an escort.

We found some of the inhabitants of Sirdhana escaping with their property on tattoos, to prevent its being plundered in the expected dacoity: when, therefore, we marched into the town, although it was scarcely daylight, we roused all the inhabitants by the *reveillée* from our bugles, fully convinced it would be a most gratifying sound to many of the poor Bunyahs. I examined the Tehsil building, and found it quite unfit for defence, being hemmed in with thatched houses, and yet not having sufficient accommodation for the detachment of the 11th Native Infantry on duty there; some of whom were living in the bazaar, and some of the new levy horsemen separated altogether from the others. The defence of the Cathedral would, moreover, be more possible from the Palace than from the Tehsil; and the destruction of the Tehsil building would he little loss to any one, while the destruction of the Palace or Cathedral would be irreparable. I therefore transferred the treasure, records, and guards to the Palace.

The Palace is placed on a pediment, about ten feet high: a broad flight of stone steps leads up to the hall-door. The principal rooms are, therefore, situated on what may be called a second story; a verandah runs along the entire front; two small raised verandahs project from each side of the house, and a Zenana, or women's inclosure, with a pucka wall around, occupied the rear. It was, of course, possible to make such a building impregnable to anything except heavy guns, and there was room in it for all the Christians in Sirdhana. I therefore had crenulated breastworks of loose bricks made in the verandahs, and at all places flanking the building. A kutcha well was dug in the compound in about eight hours, and a week's provision stored. The news of our coming to Sirdhana reached the rebels at Boorhana within three hours of our arrival. The excellence of the intelligence received by the rebels on all occasions proves them to have had many friends amongst those not committed to rebellion. We installed the detachment of fifty men of the 11th Native Infantry in the Palace, and their presence effectually protected the buildings in Sirdhana throughout the disturbances.

Chapter Ten

Though numbers of the people, both Hindoos and Mussulmans, embraced the opportunity of our Civil administration being in abeyance, to plunder indiscriminately, or even to enter with a will into rebellion, yet there were several pleasing instances of a just appreciation of the advantage of our rule. One of the most striking is that of the Rajpoot village of Solana. A portion of the Meerut district, between Haupper and Delhi, is known as Rajpootana; and at the Rajpoot village of Dhowlana in it we had a police-station, consisting of a Thannadar, a Jemadar, a Mohurrir, or writer, and twelve policemen.

The Mussulmans of the neighbourhood were all in favour of the King of Delhi, and the post became one of great danger in consequence of its distance from Meerut, and the temporary abandonment by us of the next district of Boolundshehur. The Thannadar Toraballi, though a Mussulman, remained loyal, and a reward was offered for his head by the Delhi rebels. The Rajpoots of Dhowlana itself, however, most inopportunely chose to rebel; and, attacking the Thannah, drove out all the police, taking the Thannadar prisoner, reporting the fact to Delhi, with a request for instructions as to how they were to dispose of him.

The Rajpoots of the neighbouring village of Solana then assembled, attacked their brethren of Dhowlana, released the Thannadar, and set up of their own accord the British police-station in their own village of Solana; there

Toraballi remained in safety until after the fall of Delhi.

The Dhowlana men, however, knowing that they had sinned beyond forgiveness, kept that quarter in a state of disturbance. The aspect of affairs just then about Cawnpore was anything but satisfactory; communications with the southward were closed, and the Dhowlana men incited their brethren to rise, with a promise of support from Bareilly. I therefore visited the spot, accompanied by my joint magistrate, W——, and a strong force of the military police. We hanged fourteen of the leaders of the revolt to trees in their own villages, and placed the loyalists of Solana in full possession of the village and lands of Dhowlana (with the exception of a quarter share owned by the Skinner family), a possession which I trust will be confirmed to them by Government.

News having been received at Meerut that the rebel chief of Malagurh had pushed a considerable number of his men on to Galowtee, in the Boolundshehur district, and was threatening Haupper, an expedition, consisting of two Horse Artillery guns, a troop of her Majesty's 6th Dragoon Guards, fifty of the 60th Queen's Royal Rifles, thirty of the Khakee Ressalah, thirty-five of the Meerut district Nujeebs, and twenty armed native Christians, started for that direction on the night of the 21st July, arriving at Haupper the next morning.

We there heard that Wullee Dad Khan had posted 400 Sowars and 600 infantry, besides a crowd of rebel villagers, at Galowtee, where he had fortified the police-station by breastworks. Major W——, the commandant of the Volunteers, was, as senior officer, in command of the entire party, and determined on attacking the rebels the next day at daybreak. As the place was out of my own district, and the civil officer belonging to it was with us, I went as a trooper merely in the Ressalah.

The guns with the Rifles and Nujeebs were to be in the centre, the Carbineers on the right flank, and the Khakees on the left; and as we marched "right in front," the Carbineers, of course, led the way.

On approaching a bridge, about five miles from Galowtee, some friendly Jâts announced to us that it was occupied by a picket of the enemy's cavalry, some fifty in number. They were caught, as is usually the case, napping, no videttes being thrown out; and the Carbineers, under Captain Wardlaw, charged and cut up the greater number of them, many being killed without being able to get into their saddles. The two leaders in charge of the picket, Ismael Khan and Hajee Mooneer Khan, were both wounded.

The Sowars, as they fled, fired their matchlocks over their shoulders at their assailants, but made very poor practice. One of the Carbineers was shot through the left shoulder, and several bad sword-cuts were received, but none of our men were killed. I believe that the charge of the Carbineers would have had more fatal effect, if they had used the thrust instead of cutting with their swords, as they always appeared to do.

As we moved on, a large body of Sowars, in position opposite the Thannah of Galowtee, came in sight. The guns were moved to the front, the cavalry behind them, and the Rifles in skirmishing order cleared the fields and inclosures on our flanks, as we moved along. The guns opened with round shot and shrapnel, at a short distance from the Thannah, quickly dispersing the enemy's Sowars.

The whole affair was managed in a manner highly creditable to our gallant commandant. On our entering the Thannah inclosure, we found evidence of the persevering ingenuity of the rebels in their having adapted a large quantity of the material of our electric telegraph line to the present exigencies of their position. They had dug up a number of the cast-iron socket-screws, in which the telegraph posts are placed, struck off the phlanges of the screws, bored touch-holes in them, and were mounting them as guns, on carriages.

They employed the thick telegraph-wire for fixing and strengthening them, besides cutting up a large portion of it into small lengths for grape. Two guns, with their limbers, ammunition, portfire, &c, were found, all complete. The guns were fitted with elevating-screws; but the cartridge-bags were stupidly filled with the grape and powder mixed up indiscriminately throughout the entire length of each cartridge. About seventy of the enemy altogether were killed; and, but for the extreme heat, our expedition was most useful and exciting.

The extent to which iron and brass guns, of various calibre, are buried in villages in this country, is hardly credible; but it is only when a district is abandoned, that they are dug up in numbers. Two more complete telegraph guns were, after Delhi fell, found in the Tehsil of Moradnugger, besides three small iron guns made of iron bars hooped together with rings. I also recovered two iron guns, one of very heavy metal, from the village of Boundea. They had been dug up at Purreechutghur, where they must have lain half a century, and were probably last used when Nain Sing was the Goojur King of Eastern Meerut. Mr. S———, the magistrate of Boolundshehur, found sixty guns of various calibres, in different parts of his district.

On the 18th of September, news came to Meerut that the Mussulmans of the town of Mowana had attacked certain Bunyahs' shops there, and plundered them; that the Bunyahs had called in a number of Goojurs from neighbouring villages for their protection – the sheep, in fact, calling in the wolves. But, on the other hand, their Mussulman assailants had sent round amongst the Goojurs the more pleasing invitation of joining them in a general loot of the entire bazaar. The consequence was, that in a wonderfully short space of time, several thousands of Goojurs had surrounded the town of Mowana, and the Government Tehsil building by it.

Mr. F———, of whose gallantry I have spoken, had by that time been appointed Lieutenant of the Police in the Meerut district. I therefore started with him for Mowana, taking every available man with us. Our party only numbered thirty-six Sowars and twenty footmen; but there were thirty Sepoys of the late 11th Native Infantry at the Tehsil, and we found them quite enough for the Goojurs, the latter abandoning their position as soon as they heard of the approach of regular troops, and scattering to their homes, when we took up our quarters in the Tehsil.

We had an exciting time of it, as the struggle after the assault for the city of Delhi was then going on, and the people of the district in a fever of excitement to know whether "their Raj" or ours was to triumph. I had the Tehsil building, therefore, made defensible by loop-holing it, erecting four little flanking towers, and surrounding the whole with a parapet and ditch.

On the second day after our arrival, we received stirring news from Meerut - the complete capture of Delhi, the death by cholera of Mr. Greathed, (the Governor-General's agent in camp, and late Commissioner of Meerut.) the revolt of Thannali Bhowun in the Mozuffernugger district, and the repulse of the district officer and the strong force with which he attacked it.

The Delhi victory was only what we expected. By Greathed's death, just after the assault (a most sudden and unexpected misfortune), I lost an able superior and a firm friend, and Government one of its most clear-headed and useful officers.

To a young officer, especially in the Civil department, it is of very great importance what Commissioner he acts under. There are some who, by their disinterested exertions in pushing the claims of their subordinates with Government, excite them to efforts and exploits which they never would attempt under an incompetent, inefficient, or inconsiderate superior. Such men as Henry Tucker, Montgomery, and others I could name, not only aid Government by their own individual services, but far more by the earnest zeal with which they inspire their subordinates. I firmly believe that most of the present Civil Service will do their duty, though hopeless of distinction. But there is always an additional incentive to exertion in the prospect of a recognition of your services by your superiors or fellow-countrymen. Military men can win the highest object of a soldier's ambition, "The Victoria Cross," only through the recommendation of their commanding officer. Civilians must ordinarily gain the approval of Government through their immediate superiors, though the press can often award them the approval of the public. The former an accident may deprive of; but to the latter, those who treat it openly and honourably may always look for justice and impartiality.

The defeat of the Mozuffernugger party before Thannah Bhowun was a serious matter; and as it was thought very possible that some of the mutineers flying from Delhi might join the Thannah Bhowun rebels, the column, including the Khakee Ressalah, watching Wulee Dad Khan at Haupper, was ordered off to assist the

Mozuffernugger officer. Thinking that our little clump of spears might be useful in the same direction, we rode that night a march of thirty miles to Mozuffernugger. Our Sikhs had been celebrating the fall of Delhi at the grog-shop in Mowana, and one of them was found quite unable to manage his horse, which ran away with him, knocking down and injuring two of the Nujeebs, besides causing its owner to lose his sword. I made the fellow march on foot the remainder of the way to Mozuffernugger, and he was quite sober by the time he got there. At Mozuffernugger we found a very powerful force collected, which marched the same night for Thannah Bhowun, eighteen miles distant.

As we approached the place, a Mussulman city, densely crowded with brick-built courtyards and houses, seeing some men stealing away in the distance, I got permission for the men with me, who, under the name of "Dunlop's Irregulars," were, by detachment orders, posted on the extreme right, to pursue them. We could only catch seven, who were pistolled or cut down at once; and we then swept round to surround four horsemen who appeared in a clump of trees near. Stringent orders were given to dispose of the riders without injuring the horses, as we already looked on the latter as our own: and correctly so, as it afterwards proved – for to our great disgust we found we had surrounded four of our own party.

The city was found to be completely abandoned; one single occupant, a Mussulman in a mosque, who was shot by a Sikh, being the only inhabitant. There is something startling in wandering through long streets of houses in which no human being is to be found: the deserted streets looking like those of some plague city; while on entering the houses, the pet animals and cattle, the fires burning, and food in the different residences, made it appear as if the owners had been removed by magic. Just outside the town lay a melancholy memento of the last visit to this place, – a heap of the putrefying bodies of some poor Sikhs thrown out like offal to waste away in the sun.

We wandered all day through the city, and an urgent requisition for my presence in my own district obliged me to start the same evening on my way back to Meerut, riding eighteen miles that night, and thirty-six the next. Lieutenant F——— accompanied me throughout. The horsemen with me, besides skirmishing about all day, had been up for four nights running, and marched during that time upwards of one hundred miles. It was not to be wondered at, therefore, that the horses of my skeleton troop of cavalry put on a most appropriate appearance.

The fall of Delhi called away many of the volunteers to their proper duties. There were not many left when at Thannah Bhowun; and they also were disbanded a few days afterwards. Many of these had acquired a taste for the active life they had been for some time leading, and sought congenial employ in other places. Two of the most dashing men in the second subdivision received local lieutenancies, and others enlisted in the Meerut Light Horse. One, an enormously corpulent youth, applied for employment in the forces of one of our neighbouring Rajahs, objecting, as he himself expressed it, to enter the Queen's or Company's Service, as he "couldn't abear being dummeneered over."

I must apologise, as a civilian, for offering the following hints on self-defence to my readers; but as they are deduced from practical experience, I believe they will be found useful to those who may have to undertake as unexpectedly as myself such modern moss-trooping.

For a horseman it is advisable, as a general rule, that he

should use his revolvers for footmen, and his sword for mounted enemies. An active footman is generally more than a match for a swordsman on horseback, if fighting at the time, though numbers are cut up with facility as soon as they turn and fly. This last is partly attributable to the native idiosyncrasy in apathetically yielding, when they think they have no chance, which I have before alluded to.

Very much of course depends upon your horse, and a brute that won't stand fire should never be mounted as a charger. A native cannot cope with a good fencer using the small sword, but will very likely beat him if he keeps to cutting only. There are few, however, who understand fencing; and it is advisable for such to have a light steel arm-guard made to suit the outside of the arm from the elbow to the wrist, with a slight raised catch at the elbow, and the other end projecting well out to save the fingers. Such a guard is easily fastened on by two broad leather straps to the arm. I give here a sketch of what I call "The Wallace Guard".

The Wallace Guard.

I also represent in the opposite diagram the manner of using it. As it is concealed by the sleeve of the coat, and as a good native swordsman could cut through the unprotected arm and cleave the skull with facility, he does not check or change his blow on seeing the arm raised. But at the same moment that he discovers from the jar to

Cut And Thrust.

his wrist, that "you must have had some iron under your sleeve," he finds that he has himself got something similar transfixing his own body.

On horseback it is usual for two opponents to close sword-arm to sword-arm; but when using the guard, it is better, after approaching in the usual way on nearing your adversary, to incline your horse a little to the right, so as to pass on his left. The cut any native will give is probably No. 1, or No. 6, either of which is easily received on the left arm, of course dropping the rein, and giving a cross point at the same time.

I remember on one occasion a gallant young officer nearly losing his life from accepting a challenge from a swordsman on foot. Three hundred cavalry, few of whom had any weapons but their swords, were most injudiciously sent by an old civilian, who certainly was not blessed with any intuitive knowledge of the military art, and appears to have acquired none by experience, to attack a Tehsil station in the possession of the rebels, which was surrounded by a loopholed wall, upwards of fifteen feet high, protected by flanking towers at the four corners, and filled by matchlock men. There were 500 altogether in or about the Tehsil. My joint-magistrate and myself had determined to accompany the party; for, though protesting as political officials against the folly of the plan of attack, we had some curiosity as simple troopers, although the Khakees were not to be there, to see the scrimmage, and perhaps gain a wrinkle as to how cavalry were to ride over a wall fifteen feet high, or through one two feet thick. As I did not know the hour at which the party started, we left Meerut at daylight, but found that the cavalry had left some three hours before us, and were just returning as we got near the locality of their attempt.

We first met two or three wounded men, who gave a

dismal account of the business; but from the officers, Tehsildar and others, who came up just afterwards, we had a better account. They had failed, as a matter of course, in the main object of the expedition, i.e. catching or killing the rebel Tehsildar and his myrmidons, who returned to their old position as soon as the cavalry had returned to Meerut; but the four military officers ordered out on the occasion, two of them belonging to the Mooltanee Horse and two to the 3rd Light Cavalry, had done much to make up for the deficiency or incompetency in planning the affair.

Their first attempt to get into the Serai enclosure was a failure; but they succeeded in frightening the rebel Tehsildar, who thinking, doubtless, that infantry and guns must certainly be coming, instead of remaining in Tehsil with his followers, where he could have laughed at cavalry, fled from the place; and on the cavalry returning to the attack, the loopholes not being properly manned, they dismounted, burnt down the gate, and then entered the place, killing some few of the insurgents. Young Lieutenant A——— was hailed by a swordsman on foot, who challenged him to single combat, but protested against any opponent taking the duty advantage of using pistols. Lieutenant A——— chivalrously and rashly, though he had a loaded pistol in his holster, rode at the fellow with his sword, and was severely wounded by him in three places, one cut dividing the ulnar nerve, paralysed his sword-arm, and he would certainly have been killed directly afterwards, but that one of his Mooltanee horsemen rode up and attacked the footman (rather an unfair thing in single combat, by-the-bye), saving his officer's life by killing his opponent.

Chapter Eleven

It is to be hoped that, as the number of our European community increases, a much larger proportion of Europeans will be employed in our subordinate police offices. As it is, the native policemen being much too afraid of the fists of any drunken European to arrest without wounding him, and as of course in such times it would not do to permit them the use, as they always wish, of deadly weapons, the magistrates and district officers are often obliged to undertake ordinary executive duties better suited to Private A1 of the Metropolitan or other police: they alternate, in fact, between governing a province or acting as common constables.

My assistant, young E. C———, had, on one occasion, to go out to Sirdhanah and bring back a soldier of the 60th Q. Rifles, who had installed himself at that place as a self-elected Proconsul, had compelled the native officials to clear out a house for him, levied contributions from the Bunyas, and passed his time in expatiating on his own elevated position, and parading about the bazaar, when half drunk, to the mortal terror of the Bunyas. He was delivered over to the commanding officer of his corps, but escaped again shortly afterwards from custody. At ten o'clock one night, some time after the capture of Delhi, I was called on by the Tehsildar, who is head of the native police in his own division, to report that a public conveyance running between Delhi and Meerut had been stopped near the former place, by a drunken European, who insisted on getting in, to the great alarm of two native passengers by the vehicle. He remained quiet for some time, but then commenced a personal assault on one of the passengers, whom he quickly ejected, the other abandoning his seat of his own accord. The European then ordered the coachman to drive on, expressing himself, so far as the driver could make out, perfectly indifferent as to the direction in which they went. When within five miles of Meerut, he dismissed the coachman also, preferring to drive his own conveyance. The horse being an old stager, took him straight to his stables, where he was found by the coachman, who followed on foot, dead drunk, inside of the palkie gharrie.

The usual plan is to make over such characters to the Brigade-Major, but it is not always easy to arrest them for the purpose; and as it was then late, I ordered the Tehsildar to lock the fellow up in some strong room in the Tehsil till morning, his intoxication rendering him helpless. This was duly done; but at two o'clock I was awoke by an urgent express from the Tehsildar, to the effect that the Feringhee had grown furious, and was expected shortly to kick his way through the door of his cell. It was evident he could not have been so drunk as at first supposed. Having no agency fitted for the duty, I hurried down myself, and found a brawny European soldier of the 2d Company's Fusiliers, with a most Donnybrook appearance, and considerably intoxicated. He would not then; however, let me know his name or regiment. I tried reasoning with him at first, offering him the choice of remaining where he was till the morning, or going at once before the Brigade-Major, telling him that he should not be released until I had learnt what had become of the Dawk travellers. Neither alternative suited him; and so refusing to do either, he swore that if restrained at all, he would take some one's life before he left.

One only of the Chuprassies on foot, and four of my Sikh guard on horseback, had remained to see the door of his cell opened, the others having a ludicrous dread of its occupant. After conversing rationally some time, he suddenly flew at the unfortunate footman, dealing him a blow on the face, and started off, pursued by myself. The Tehsildar unfortunately coming in his way, was collared; and as I had not the usual bâton with which such a character would receive an anodyne application on the head from a London policeman, I had to take my friend by the throat, and commence a simple trial of strength between a sober man and a tipsy one. The Sikhs, however, promptly dismounted, and, coming to my assistance, pinioned the culprit hand and foot. He howled and struggled like a wild beast, but was marched off "vi et armis" to the Brigade-Major's, indulging in a torrent of abuse, and exhibiting considerable fertility of resource in the variety and, to me at least, novelty of his invectives. At one time, in contradistinction to the social position which he was pleased to ascribe to me, he announced himself to be an Irishman, one of the finest soldiers in creation. "Och! we're the pride of the world, we are," he said. This gratifying reflection appeared to mollify him considerably, but the flattering unction was so frequently applied that it began to lose its effect, and he returned with renewed vigour to execration and abuse. As I would do nothing but smile blandly at the confidential communications as to his personal opinion of my eyes, limbs, and relations, with which he favoured me, he tried the effect of translating his select sentences into not very select Hindoostani, for the information and improvement of the natives around, and I was glad to deposit him in the quarter guard of H. M. 6th Dragoons, to be disposed of by the military authorities.

The continuance or gradual extinction of the

covenanted Civil Service of India, is a question which the disturbances of the last twelve months will probably do much to solve; and though the individual members of that service have honourably sustained the name for high moral courage, and its inferior virtue, British pluck, which distinguishes throughout the world the class from which they are drawn, viz. the "younger sons" and gentlemen of home society, yet it has now outlived the exigencies of its former organisation. It will do more good as a less exclusive body, and its monopoly will, it is to be hoped, die out amidst the reforms which our present military necessities have engendered. There are certain departments of Treasury, Auditorship and Account, the branches of a superior kind of clerkship, for which many of those now known as uncovenanted civilians, are by their training and experience eminently qualified, and in which many of the hard-working officers of our present highly-educated Civil Service would find useful and congenial employ; but the Commissionerships in all their grades throughout India should be differently filled.

Lord Ellenborough, when Governor-General, made some suggestions on the subject, which, like many others of his almost epigrammatic projects for reform, after-experience has shown to have been flashes of true genius: "he sprang," in fact, "to the truth at a bound." He is said to have hinted that our home nominations, whether the vacancies are civil or military, should be to the army. There are now many in the Civil Service whose natural bent would have kept them in the military branch, and who would have been infinitely more useful there than in their present posts. There are many officers moreover in the army, who would make admirable administrative *employés*, but who cannot be employed through want of vacancies. A knowledge of military discipline and science is often of great service to an Indian administrator; while all district officers of experience can testify how true is the converse of the position, as to a knowledge of the people and civil duties, to officers in high military command. The difference is striking between soldiers under the command of such men as Brigadier Coke and others, who know by experience the heavy labours and responsibilities of district officials, and those under the command of bigoted regimental officers, who since their school-days, having received little enlightenment beyond the literature of the manual and platoon, look to their own hazy views of Civil science as the perfection of reason; who deem the people made for them and their men, not themselves servitors of the public, and whose correspondence with the civil authorities often assumes, especially under the delusion of that "unknown quantity," martial law, an unnecessary defiant tone, which they adopt as a protest against civil superiority, and a declaration of their own dignity and importance.

I noticed in the Lahore Chronicle of the 17th April, 1858, the following passage, quoted from a letter to the Englishman, from one of the ever-glorious garrison of Lucknow.

"There are instances wherein the brutal licence of martial law was equally perilous to the native rebel in arms and to the European civilian. It is notorious that the presence of Mr. Gubbins ameliorated the position of the uncovenanted members of the public service subjected to the capricious ferocities of certain military dispensers of justice during the eventful siege of the Residency of Lucknow. It is not too much to affirm that the code of the Orderly Room is not applicable in all cases to the redress of civil grievances. It is not too much to say that martial law dispensed by men to whom the very forms and procedure of civil justice are offensive, can degenerate into abuse."

The writer of the above would not, I believe, have had such experience to record, had the military authorities of Lucknow therein referred to, had their share of Civil training. The present system of examination for the Civil Service has notoriously failed in bringing the best class of men to this country, and the army has fully earned by its noble services and sufferings some great and imperial gift from our country. Our true policy is unquestionably to choose one man from a class that can be trusted, such as those from which the officers of our army are drawn; let them all pass, not a competitive but a standard examination, and let the practical test of how they turn out in this country determine the character of their employment. We shall do better, I imagine, by following among Asiatics the more vigorous system of continental Europe, than by borrowing from the pseudo-civilisation of China. To give full scope to this system, however, both military and civil employ must remain open throughout to the nominees, and we must at the same time devise means to prevent the dissatisfaction and disgust which supposed neglect formerly caused among regimental officers hopeless of staff employ.

This might, however, easily be regulated, by allowing those who enjoyed the emoluments and did the work of civil administration, to count, while so engaged, only one year towards military rank for every two of service. By this means the regimental officer who devoted himself to military duty, would gradually pass in military rank over his more fortunate senior on civil duty; while the latter, if he returned to his corps for active service, or for any other cause, would return to a place in the regiment better suited to his limited regimental experience, than that which under the present system is unjustly enjoyed.

The brunt of the outbreak has fallen on the North-West and Oude, and the civilians of this Presidency have suffered more severely than any other class of men in the country. There were in our Presidency, when the mutiny commenced, 153 civilians, about one-third of whom have been killed or wounded, i.e. twenty-nine have been murdered, killed in action, or died of wounds; three died from cholera, from exposure on service, and several have been wounded. I may not know all. I can detail the following list of the dead; but I do not attempt to give the names of the wounded, as it is difficult to correct the list without some official record, and the Gazettes take no notice of civilians' wounds.

Died of Cholera.

J. R. Colvin.

H. H. Greathed

W. C. Watson.

Murdered, killed in action, or died of their wounds.

D. Robertson.	G. D. Raikes.
C. W. Moore.	H. E. Cockerell.
C. G. Hillersdon.	J. R. Mackillop.
S. Fraser.	J. R. Hutchinson.
A. Galloway.	W. Clifford.
D. Grant.	J. Wedderburn.
B. R Cuppage.	P. Macwhirter.
M. Ricketts.	A. C. Smith.

M. C. Ommany.   G. J. Christian.

H. B. Thornhill.   R. B. Thornhill.

R. N. Lewis.   R. J. Tucker.

F. K. Lloyd   G. Thomason.

H. Gonne.   R. H. G. Black.

J. B. Thornhill.   Sir M. Jackson.

A. Johnston, killed by a fall from his horse.

Chapter Twelve

A conquered nation naturally discusses the chances of independence; and the Mussulmans of India, born to intrigue, and possessing an unity, of action among themselves which the Hindoos have not, have constantly been engaged in plotting our destruction. All inquiries since the disturbances tend to prove that the fomenters of this mutiny, the inventors and propagators of the falsehoods regarding the greasing of our new cartridges with cow's and pig's fat, and mixing bone dust with flour in bazars, were Mussulmans.

The following facts will prove that, though the exact locality of the first outbreak was not arranged, though the train took light unexpectedly, a mutiny of the army, and a Mussulman rebellion, were planned and fully expected. In the service of the Begum Sombre at Sirdhanah were several foreigners, French, Italians, and Germans. They appear to assimilate more readily with the people of the country they inhabit than Englishmen, and most of them had half-caste families at Sirdhanah. These descendants are Roman Catholic Christians, whose interests, being identical with our own, have often been found useful in subordinate police posts. One of these, François Sisten, was, before the mutiny, Thanadar, or Police Inspector, at Seetapore, in Oude. He had got three months' leave, came to see his family in Meerut and some friends in Saharunpore, and called on the joint-magistrate of that place, Mr. R. Edwardes, to pay his respects. He was sitting native fashion in an ante-room of Mr. Edwardes' house with other police employés, when a Mussulman Tehsildar of the Bijnour district entered the room. Sisten was dressed, as usual, in native clothes; he buttoned his muzaie (a sort of jacket) on the left breast, as Mussulmans do, the Hindoos buttoning it on the right. He appeared, in fact, to be a Mussulman, and, as the Tehsildar glanced at him, he inquired what service he held, and where. Sisten replied, he was a Thanadar on leave from Oude. "What news from Oude?" said the Tehsildar; "how does the work progress, brother?" "If we have work in Oude, your Highness will know it well," replied Sisten, who inherited a good deal of Hindoostanee suspicion, and made the Tehsildar thus think him not ignorant but cautious. The trifling mutinies at Barrackpore, as they were then thought, had commenced. "Depend upon it, we will succeed this time," said the Tehsildar; "the direction of the business is in able hands." Now that Tehsildar was the Nawab Ahmud Oollah Khan of Nugeenah, nephew of the Nawab Mahmood Khan of Nujeebabad, and is, or was on the 1st of May, the leader of the rebels in Bijnour; but had Sisten reported, as he himself says, such a conversation as a matter of importance, he would at that time have been laughed at as an alarmist.

The Sepoys, the armed Budmashes of our towns, the predatory tribes, and many of the Mussulmans, were rebels or mutineers during the disturbances; on the other hand, most of the Hindoos – the principal Hindoo chiefs as a rule – declared for, and fought faithfully on the side of Government. Some few Mussulmans also showed an extraordinary and persevering attachment to a cause, which must be supposed adverse to all their natural and religious sympathies.

A peculiarly cautious policy which despises guerilla warfare, and attempts to do almost everything by one enormous army, has protracted the struggle in this country to an extent which has very seriously increased the injury to our *prestige*. Of the final result, however, none can be doubtful; and the security of the empire lies in our own hands.

If we have none but European Artillery and regular troops, and enforce most strictly and universally the disarming orders for all but Europeans and servants of Government, our country will have gained greatly by the disasters which have caused us the loss of so many of our relatives and friends; but if a negligent apathy allows matters to take very much their former channel, we shall not, in another mutiny, have the same assistance from the neutrality of the people, and shall do our best to accomplish Sir Thomas Munro's prophecy, that, "Ere long, a mutiny of the Sepoy army must take place, which we shall crush; but it will be followed by a rebellion which will crush us." The conciliation policy, which many carelessly conclude has failed, is the only one which, for a time at least, can prevent our expulsion from the country. It may, however, be, and has been, forced into a folly.

I trust the insight this revolt will give our English friends into the weak and childish but cruel and treacherous native character, may prevent the mistake of legislating for them for the present at least as our equals. It is not conversion to Christianity and education of the first generation alone which can raise the Hindoostani to a par with the Anglo-Saxon. Whatever fireside philanthropists may assert, the truths of metaphysics and physiology are verified in the case of the Asiatic.

We can impart ennobling qualities to races by generations of culture, as we impart hereditary excellences by instruction to our aids of the lower animal creation. The murders of English women and children do not, it is to be hoped, require to be attended by mutilation to excite the indignation of Englishmen.

It is a patent fact, that the proud contempt which the Anglo-Saxon bears to the Asiatic has proved, to a great extent, the salvation of our Indian Empire. Nearly all men come to this country fully prepared to accord equal rights and privileges to its dusky inhabitants; but whether in the case of the civilian, the officer, or the private soldier, experience leads to but a common conviction of their debasement. Let it be our glorious task to raise them, by generations of patient effort, to our own level, but do not let us commit the folly of declaring them to be, and acting as if they were, what they are not. Many of our successes have been won almost in defeat by small bodies of our brothers, by that despite of our enemies which knew no dread of numbers, and closed at once with the rebels where ever found. Pull many of that band to whose lot it has fallen to uphold England's honour during the past crisis, have, to use a native expression, "carried their lives in their hands," and proudly hurled them, like "the Douglas heart," in the midst of England's enemies, content to defend them successfully, or lose them in that cause which a handful of our countrymen upheld for six months against the hosts which joined our rebel army.

We have in our enormous empire various distinct tribes, whom, up to the present time, we have in blind confidence kept to guard their native provinces, to rivet the chains of the conquest of their own people. Why should we continue a system so fraught with danger, when the solution of a problem has been given us by Austria, which we can demonstrate so much more completely out here? Why are not the Sepoys of the British Government invariably aliens to the people, and strangers to the country in which they are employed? It is not our proper policy to amalgamate the races under us, or to mix them in regiments, but to keep the nationality of our tribes as distinct and complete as possible; but then none but recruiting depots of Sikh corps should remain in the Punjab. General service corps of Punjabees would be invaluable in Bengal and Madras; the low castes of Bombay, in Oude or the North-West; while the most mutinous of our Poorbeah corps might, when the country resumed its normal quiet, be our most active and able allies on the Peshawer frontier.

It is to be hoped that our home counsels are not like those of the Bourbons, which will neither learn or forget anything; that the folly of communicating every improvement in warfare to our conquered subjects, entrusting them with every discovery in science, and the same weapons used by Europeans, may not again be committed; and that enthusiastic officers may not be allowed to arm and discipline native corps with the express object of attaining to the boast, that they are nearly equal to our own regiments. A time will, doubtless, come, when we may in full confidence impart to all on the Peninsula every improvement or discovery we possess; but it will not be till the native Christian community equals or outnumbers every other; when that harvest appears for which hundreds of earnest-minded labourers, in trusting faith, have sown, and the results of which we know are as certain as the truths of our religion.

When revolving before the mind's eye the stirring events of the past year, and even excluding altogether the daily budget of news, whether of Anglo-Saxon heroism, or of Sepoy atrocities on defenceless womanhood and helpless infancy, there is enough of incident at almost any district in India, to afford material for a much longer sketch than the present. It is only difficult for an actor in the scenes described to omit what is redundant. I have attempted to seize on salient and characteristic incidents, chiefly to contribute some details of the origin and local character of the disturbance, as an atom of fact for the future help of history.

We have still before us the important work of inflicting a stern and retributive justice on those who have so lately deluged India with English blood. Let us trust that our countrymen, however, those especially who hold the responsible post of Special Commissioners, may not be tempted by the promise of a bastard reputation, to a careless or indiscriminate system of punishment, by which our friends must suffer as well as our foes. They should fearlessly force the truth, as regards native debasement, through the fallacies of philanthropists at home, and as fearlessly protect and defend many of the natives whom it is their duty to support against the folly of sham heroic injustice or severity out here. Let us act as those who know that we are not only servants of the British Government, but ministers of that God to whom justice and mercy, as well as vengeance, belongeth; that we shall all one day stand, our enemies and their victims, ourselves and the men now almost daily sentenced for execution, before an unerring and all-wise Judgment Seat, where the plea of natural or national prejudice will not bar judgment for false stewardship, the term of which judgment extends to eternity.

Appendix
List Of Corps That Have Mutinied Or Been Disarmed.

★ Partially mutinied.

† The 4th Troop mutinied at Jelpigoree, and the 3d Troop at Madargunge.

‡ Excepting the 2d and 3d Companies.

§ Remaining 6 Companies Disarmed at Raneegunge.

§§ The other 3 Companies mutinied at Chittagong.

Corps.		Mutinied or Disarmed	Station
5th Light Field Battery. 6th		Mutinied	Delhi
6th	Ditto	Ditto	Nusserabad
13th	Ditto	Ditto	Fyzabad, Oude
15th	Ditto	Ditto	Bareilly
18th	Ditto	Ditto	Nowgong
4th Troop 1st B. H. A		Ditto	Neemuch
2d Co. 7th Bat. Artillery		Ditto	Nusseerabad
3th " 7th	Ditto	Ditto	Delhi
5th " 7th	Ditto	Ditto	Fyzabad, Oude
6th " 7th	Ditto	Ditto	Cawnpore
1st " 8th	Ditto	Ditto	Cawnpore
2d " 8th	Ditto	Ditto	Lucknow
3d " 8th	Ditto	Disbanded	Almorale

Corps.	Mutinied or Disarmed	Station
6th " 8th Ditto	Mutinied	Bareilly
4th " 9th Ditto	Ditto	Nowgong
2d " 9th★ Ditto	Ditto	Dacca
6th " 9th★ Ditto	Ditto	Azimgurh, Allahabad
Sappers and Miners	Ditto	Roorkee
G. G. Body Guard	Disarmed	Calcutta
1sr Light Cavalry	Mutinied	Mhow, Neemuch
2d Light Cavalry	Ditto	Cawnpore
3d Ditto	Ditto	Meerut
4th Ditto	Disarmed	Umballah
5th Ditto	Ditto	Peshawer
6th★ Ditto	Mutinied	Jullunder
7th★ Ditto	Ditto	Lucknow
8th Ditto	Disarmed	Lahore
9th★ Ditto	Mutinied	Sealkote
10th★ Ditto	Ditto	Ferozepore
1st Native Infantry	Ditto	Cawnpore
2d Ditto	Disarmed	Barrackpore
3d Ditto	Mutinied	Phillour, Loodianah
4th Ditto	Disarmed	Noorpoor, Kangra
5th Ditto	Mutinied	Umballah
6th Ditto	Ditto	Allahabad, Futtehpore

Corps.			Mutinied or Disarmed	Station
7th	Ditto		Ditto	Dinapore
8th	Ditto		Ditto	Dinapore
9th	Ditto		Ditto	Allygurh, Boolundshehur, Etawah, Mynpoorie
10th	Ditto		Ditto	Futtehgurh
11th	Ditto		Ditto	Meerut
12th	Ditto		Ditto	Nowgong, Jhansi
13th★	Ditto		Ditto	Lucknow
14th	Ditto		Ditto	Jhelum
15th	Ditto		Ditto	Nusseerabad
16th	Ditto		Disarmed	Lahore, Goojerat
17th‡	Ditto		Mutinied	Azimgurh
18th	Ditto		Ditto	Bareilly
19th	Ditto		Disbanded	Barrackpore
20th	Ditto		Mutinied	Meerut
22th	Ditto		Ditto	Fyzabad, Oude
23d	Ditto		Ditto	Mhow
24th	Ditto		Disarmed	Peshawer
25th	Ditto	Wing	Ditto	Benares
26th	Ditto		Mutinied	Lahore
27th	Ditto		Disarmed	Peshawer
28th	Ditto		Mutinied	Shahjehanpore
29th	Ditto		Ditto	Moradabad

Corps.			Mutinied or Disarmed	Station
30th	Ditto		Ditto	Nusseerabad, Ajmere, Jeypore
32d	Ditto	Detach	Ditto	Deogurh, Rampore, Haut §
33d	Ditto		Disarmed	Hooshjarpore
34th	Ditto		{ 7 Companies disbanded }	Barrackpore §§
35th Native Infantry			Disarmed	Sealkote, Shahpore, Goojranwallah, Goojerat
36th	Ditto		Mutinied	Jullunder
37th★	Ditto		Ditto	Benares
38th	Ditto		Ditto	Delhi
39th	Ditto		Disarmed	Dehree Ishmeal Khan
40th	Ditto		Mutinied	Dinapore
41st	Ditto		Ditto	Seetapore, Mullaon
42d★	Ditto		Ditto	Saugor
43d	Ditto		Disarmed	Barrackpore
44th	Ditto		{ Disarmed and Dispersed }	Agra, Mutera
45th	Ditto		Mutinied	Ferozepore
46th	Ditto		Ditto	Sealkote
47th	Ditto		Disarmed	Mirzapore

Corps.		Mutinied or Disarmed	Station
48th★	Ditto	Mutinied	Lucknow
49th	Ditto	Disarmed	Lahore
50th★	Ditto	Mutinied	Nagode
51st	Ditto	Ditto	Peshawer
52d	Ditto	Ditto	Jubbulpore
53d	Ditto	Ditto	Cawnpore, Oude
54th	Ditto	Ditto	Delhi
53th	Ditto	Ditto	Nowshera
56th	Ditto	Ditto	Cawnpore, Banda
57th	Ditto	Ditto	Ferozepore
58th	Ditto	Disarmed	Rawul Pindee
59th	Ditto	Ditto	Umritzer
60th	Ditto	Mutinied	Rohtuck
61st	Ditto	Ditto	Jullunder
62d	Ditto	Disarmed	Mooltan
63d	Ditto	Ditto	Berharnpore
64th	Ditto	Ditto	Peshawer, Forts Mackeson, Barrah
65th	Ditto	Ditto	Ghazeepore
67th	Ditto	{ Disarmed and dispersed }	Agra, Mutera
68th	Ditto	Mutinied	Bareilly
69th	Ditto	Disarmed	Mooltan
70th	Ditto	Ditto	Barrackpore

Corps.		Mutinied or Disarmed	Station
71st*	Ditto	Mutinied	Lucknow
72d	Ditto	Ditto	Neemuoh
73d	Ditto	Ditto	Dacca
74th	Ditto	Ditto	Delhi
Regiment of Loodianah		Mutinied in part	Juanpore
Calcutta Militia		Disarmed	Allypore
Banighur Battalion*		Mutinied	Chota, Nagpore
Hurrianah Light Infan		Ditto	Hansi, Sirsa, Hissar
3d Irregular Cavalry		Ditto	Saugor
4th*	Ditto	Ditto	Hansi, Sirsa, Hissar
5th	Ditto	Ditto	Bhangulpore
7th	Ditto	Disarmed	Peshawer
8th	Ditto	Mutinied	Bareilly
9th*	Ditto	Ditto	Proceeding to Bunnoo
10th	Ditto	Disbanded	Nowshera
11th†	Ditto	Disarmed	Berhampore
12th	Ditto	Mutinied	Segowlee
13th*	Ditto	Ditto	Benares
14th	Ditto	Ditto	Jhansi, Nowgong
15th	Ditto	Ditto	Sultanpore, Seetapore, Fyzabad

Corps.	Mutinied or Disarmed	Station
	Oude Irregular Force	
No. 1 Battery	Mutinied	Secrora
2 Ditto	Ditto	Lucknow
3 Ditto	Ditto	Ditto
4 th Ditto	Ditto	Ditto
1st Cavalry	Ditto	Secrora
2d Ditto	Ditto	Lucknow
3d Ditto	Ditto	Pertaubgurh, Secrora
1st Infantry	Ditto	Persadeepore
2d Ditto	Ditto	Secrora, Baraitch
3d Ditto	Ditto	Gonda
4th Ditto	Ditto	Lucknow
5th Ditto	Ditto	Durriabad
6th Ditto	Ditto	Fyzabad
7th Ditto	Ditto	Lucknow
8th Ditto	Ditto	Sultanpore
9th Ditto	Ditto	Seetapore
10th Ditto	Ditto	Mullaon
	Gwalior Contgent	
1st Company Artillery	Mutinied	Seepree
2d Ditto	Ditto	Gwalior
3d Ditto	Ditto	Augur
4th Dito	Ditto	Gwalior

Corps.	Mutinied or Disarmed	Station
1st Cavalry Regiment	Mutinied	Gwalior, Goonah
2d Ditto	Ditto	Augur
1st Infantry Regiment	Ditto	Gwalior
2d Ditto	Ditto	Gwalior
3d Ditto	Ditto	Seepree
4th Ditto	Ditto	Gwalior
5th Ditto	Ditto	Augur
6th Ditto	Ditto	Jubbulpore
7th Ditto	Ditto	Neerauch
Malwall Contingent	Ditto	Mehidpore
Kotah Ditto	Ditto	Agra
Bhopal Ditto	Ditto	Sehore
Joudpore Legion	Ditto	Erinpoorah

The non-commissioned officers and men of the 9th Battalion Artillery, present at Dum Dum, disarmed.

The Syce drivers, attached to No. 3 Light Field Battery, disarmed.

Explanation Of Terms

Ressaldar – A Native Captain of Irregular Cavalry.

Tehsildar – The Native Collector of a District.

Thannadar – Head of a Police District.

Budmash signifies simply a bad character; but is generally applied to the loose characters without regular occupation, ready to turn their hands to anything irregular, honest or otherwise - perhaps the latter for preference.

Nujeebs – Soldiers that are not disciplined.

Pulladars – People who carry grain.

Parushnath – In lieu of Parnshnath.

Acharuj is only a sort of Brahmin.

Havildar – Serjeant of Native Infantry.

Brinjara merchants – Travelling Grain-dealers, who almost invariably travel in very large parties.

Pergunnah – District.

Babooghur – In lieu of Babooljhur.

Mahajuns – Bankers.

Bunyahs – Grain-dealers.

Khakee – Earthy, or earth-coloured.

Five Biswa – Five-twentieths.

Chowkee – A Police-station.

Huveilie – A House.

Bahadoor – A Hero.

Palkie Gharree – Palanquin Carriage.

Jezails – Wall-pieces.

Lumbardars – Zemindars.

Zemindars – Proprietors of Land.

Jumma – Revenue.

Lumbardar – Chief Zemindar.

Russud – Supplies.

Chowrassee Dês – Eighty-four Villages.

Thakoor – A Chief.

Kutcha – Without Stone-work.

Pucka – Made with Stones.

Jemadar – A Lieutenant.

Loot – Plunder.

The End.

ALSO FROM LEONAUR
AVAILABLE IN SOFTCOVER OR HARDCOVER WITH DUST JACKET

EW1 EYEWITNESS TO WAR SERIES
RIFLEMAN COSTELLO
by Edward Costello

The Adventures of a Soldier of the 95th (Rifles) in the
Peninsula & Waterloo Campaigns of the Napoleonic Wars.

SOFTCOVER : **ISBN** 1-84677-000-9
HARDCOVER : **ISBN** 1-84677-018-1

SF1 CLASSIC SCIENCE FICTION SERIES
BEFORE ADAM & Other Stories
by Jack London

Volume 1 of The Collected Science Fiction & Fantasy
of Jack London.

SOFTCOVER : **ISBN** 1-84677-008-4
HARDCOVER : **ISBN** 1-84677-015-7

SF2 CLASSIC SCIENCE FICTION SERIES
THE IRON HEEL & Other Stories
by Jack London

Volume 2 of The Collected Science Fiction & Fantasy
of Jack London.

SOFTCOVER : **ISBN** 1-84677-004-1
HARDCOVER : **ISBN** 1-84677-011-4

SF3 CLASSIC SCIENCE FICTION SERIES
THE STAR ROVER & Other Stories
by Jack London

Volume 3 of The Collected Science Fiction & Fantasy
of Jack London.

SOFTCOVER : **ISBN** 1-84677-006-8
HARDCOVER : **ISBN** 1-84677-013-0

ALSO FROM LEONAUR
AVAILABLE IN SOFTCOVER OR HARDCOVER WITH DUST JACKET

RGW2 RECOLLECTIONS OF THE GREAT WAR 1914-18
WITH THE IMPERIAL CAMEL CORPS IN THE GREAT WAR
by Geoffrey Inchbald

The Story of a Serving Officer with the British 2nd Battalion Against the Senussi and During the Palestine Campaign.

SOFTCOVER : **ISBN** 1-84677-006-7
HARDCOVER : **ISBN** 1-84677-012-2

MC1 THE MILITARY COMMANDER SERIES
JOURNALS OF ROBERT ROGERS OF THE RANGERS
by Robert Rogers

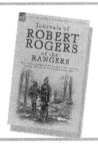

The Exploits of Rogers & the Rangers in his Own Words During 1755-1761 in the French & Indian War.

SOFTCOVER : **ISBN** 1-84677-002-5
HARDCOVER : **ISBN** 1-84677-010-6

EW2 EYEWITNESS TO WAR SERIES
CAPTAIN OF THE 95th (RIFLES)
by Jonathan Leach

An Officer of Wellington's Sharpshooters During the Peninsula, South of France and Waterloo Campaigns of the Napoleonic Wars.

SOFTCOVER : **ISBN** 1-84677-001-7
HARDCOVER : **ISBN** 1-84677-016-5

WF1 THE WARFARE FICTION SERIES
NAPOLEONIC WAR STORIES
by Sir Arthur Quiller-Couch

Tales of Soldiers, Spies, Battles & Sieges from the Peninsula & Waterloo Campaigns.

SOFTCOVER : **ISBN** 1-84677-003-3
HARDCOVER : **ISBN** 1-84677-014-9